How to
Form a Group

Other Books in the Group Work Practice Kit

What Is Group Work? (9781483332314)

Effective Planning for Groups (9781483332307)

Groups: Fostering a Culture of Change (9781483332284)

How to Select and Apply Change Strategies in Groups (9781483332277)

How to Help Leaders and Members Learn from Their Group Experience
(9781483332260)

How Leaders Can Assess Group Counseling (9781483332253)

Groups in Community and Agency Settings (9781483332246)

Group Work in Schools (9781483332239)

I dedicate this book to my favorite group—my family:
Bob, Suzanne, Zack, and Lucy the dog.

—Lynn S. Rapin

I dedicate my work to my family, teachers, and
colleagues, as we all live and work within groups as a
part of daily life.

—Jeri L. Crowell

How to Form a Group

Lynn S. Rapin
Private Practice, Cincinnati

Jeri L. Crowell
Core Faculty, Capella University
Private Practice, Macon

Los Angeles | London | New Delhi
Singapore | Washington DC

Los Angeles | London | New Delhi
Singapore | Washington DC

FOR INFORMATION:

SAGE Publications, Inc.
2455 Teller Road
Thousand Oaks, California 91320
E-mail: order@sagepub.com

SAGE Publications Ltd.
1 Oliver's Yard
55 City Road
London EC1Y 1SP
United Kingdom

SAGE Publications India Pvt. Ltd.
B 1/I 1 Mohan Cooperative Industrial Area
Mathura Road, New Delhi 110 044
India

SAGE Publications Asia-Pacific Pte. Ltd.
3 Church Street
#10-04 Samsung Hub
Singapore 049483

Acquisitions Editor: Kassie Graves
Editorial Assistant: Elizabeth Luizzi
Production Editor: Brittany Bauhaus
Copy Editor: Megan Granger
Typesetter: C&M Digitals (P) Ltd.
Proofreader: Rae-Ann Goodwin
Indexer: Marilyn Augst
Cover Designer: Anupama Krishnan
Marketing Manager: Shari Countryman

Copyright © 2014 by SAGE Publications, Inc.

Printed in the United States of America

Library of Congress Cataloging-in-Publication Data

A catalog record of this book is available from the Library of Congress.

9781483332291

This book is printed on acid-free paper.

13 14 15 16 17 10 9 8 7 6 5 4 3 2 1

Brief Contents _____

ACKNOWLEDGMENTS   ix

Chapter 1: Introduction to Group Formation   1

Chapter 2: Organize   13

Chapter 3: Market Group and Recruit Members   25

Chapter 4: Screen   31

Chapter 5: Select   39

Chapter 6: Compose   45

Chapter 7: Case Examples   51

REFERENCES   63

INDEX   71

ABOUT THE AUTHORS   75

_____ Detailed Contents

ACKNOWLEDGMENTS   ix

Chapter 1: Introduction to Group Formation   1
  Ecology of a Group   2
  Overview of Formation Steps   4
    Organize   4
    Market and Recruit   4
    Screen   5
    Select   5
    Compose   5
  Theoretical and Conceptual Support   5
    Broad Counseling Documents   6
    Broad Social Work Document   9
    Broad Psychology Document   9
    Group Specialty Documents   10
  Learning Exercise   12

Chapter 2: Organize   13
  Professional Context and Regulatory
    Requirements   13
  Resources   14
    Time   14
    The Six Ms   15
      Management Support   15
      Manpower   17
      Materials   17
      Methods and Machines 19
      Money   20
    Ethics   20
    Scope of Practice   21
    Supervision   23
  Learning Exercise   24

Chapter 3: Market Group and Recruit Members   25

  Market   25

    Planning Group   25

    Marketing to Managed Care   26

    Site-Specific Variables   27

  Recruit   28

    Referrals   29

    Recruiting Minors   29

  Learning Exercise   30

Chapter 4: Screen   31

  Role Play   33

  Interviews   33

    Components of Interviews   34

  Direct Sampling of Relevant Behavior   34

  Screening Minors   35

  Information About the Leader   36

  Research-Based Screening Instruments   36

    Group Selection Questionnaire   36

    Learning Style Inventory   37

  Learning Exercise   37

Chapter 5: Select   39

  Selection Instruments   40

  Learning Exercise   44

Chapter 6: Compose   45

  Open vs. Closed Groups   45

  Learning Exercise   47

Chapter 7: Case Examples   51

  Forming Study Groups   51

  Organize   53

    Ecological Background   53

    Resources   54

      Time   54

      Management Support   54

      Manpower   54

      Materials   54

      Methods   55

      Money   55

  Market and Recruit   55

  Screen   55

  Select   55

  Compose   56

  Case Example: Working With Street Women   56

Organize   57

    Ecological Background   57

    Resources   57

        Time   57

        Management Support   57

        Manpower   58

        Materials   58

        Methods   58

        Machines   59

        Money   59

    Market and Recruit   59

    Screen   60

    Select   60

    Compose   60

    Learning Exercise   60

    Concluding Thoughts   62

REFERENCES   63

INDEX   71

ABOUT THE AUTHORS   75

Acknowledgments_____

I wish to acknowledge mentors, colleagues, and organization participants who have enriched my life and group skills throughout my career. These include the group specialists at the University of Illinois, colleagues at Illinois State University who infused group work into the fabric of the Counseling Center, great friends in counseling and psychology, and individuals and organizations with whom I have done group interventions. Three individuals stand out: Al Dye for his modeling as the consummate group leader; Bob Conyne as model scholar and life companion; and Jeri Crowell, who has moved seamlessly from student to colleague, collaborator, and friend.

—Lynn S. Rapin

Particularly special to my own group work training was the kit to which my mentor, Bob Conyne, often referred and through which I learned the art of group leadership with his guidance. I also appreciate Lynn Rapin, my former professor and my friend, who graciously invited me to join with her to write this book. My warmest thanks go to Lynn for her calm and encouraging presence in my work, and her collaborative spirit that allowed me to fully participate in this venture as a colleague, no longer a student. As always, my family and friends loved and supported me throughout this effort, and for that I offer my sincerest gratitude.

—Jeri L. Crowell

1 Introduction to Group Formation

This book addresses practical challenges group leaders face in group formation and strategies to address them. If you have developed a group plan, you have completed just the first of many complex steps in conducting a successful group. You are now ready to consider formation of your group. Taking the time to invest in this second part of the planning phase of group work will assist you in successfully enacting your plan in the performing and processing phases.

Group workers come from different professions—for example, psychology, counseling, and social work. Within these professions are innumerable theoretical orientations and specializations. If you are reading this book or book series as a part of a graduate academic program, you and your fellow students are likely to have diverse mental health training perspectives. Students in graduate programs in the same profession may have no group courses—for example, in psychology (Barlow, 2012); one course in group dynamics—for example, in counseling, where one course is the mode (Wilson, Rapin, & Haley-Banez, 2004); or several courses and practica in group work. Therefore, it is safe to assume that there will be great variety in the training, philosophies, and experience levels of group colleagues. This can be an advantage, because group workers represent great diversity and depth of professions. On the other hand, the variety can lead to false assumptions about the training and experience of peers in the same work setting.

Planning is a best practice of group specialists and includes considerations for group formation that touch on all aspects of the ecology of the plan (Thomas & Pender, 2008). Conyne, Crowell, and Newmeyer (2008) described a group plan as a "living document" (p. 42), with potential for modification to meet the evolving needs of the group. Considerations include who will be involved, who will serve as facilitators and how many will serve, and what resources will be available, including any funding (Herner & Higgins, 2000). Organizing an approach in the planning stages often results in an increased probability of success. Conyne, Rapin, and Rand (2008) highlighted the importance of competencies that are established prior to the group meeting and additionally offer clarity in the group context for improved success.

A good idea for a group is insufficient without significant preparation to facilitate successful implementation (Corey, Corey, & Corey, 2010; Johnson & Johnson, 2003). With so many types of groups—from families to sports teams to business or industrial organizational meetings—effective characteristics are most evident when group leaders have knowledge of group dynamics and skills in managing groups. In group leaders' planning, practical details are important. Even before all the practical considerations of where, when, and with whom, for example, attention must be paid to the theoretical orientation of the group's purpose; leaders' skills and knowledge in group leadership; the rationale for choosing a group formation to address the identified issue; the objectives for the group work; and the topics, activities, and group techniques to be explored with group members, even the procedures for evaluating how well the group is doing as time goes on (Jacobs, Masson, & Harvill, 2009).

Ecology of a Group

An ecosystem comprises "a complex group of interdependent living beings . . . , which are constantly interacting with one another and take advantage of this interaction" (Chukhray, 2012, p. 13). Likewise, a group of people is made up of complex individuals interacting and creating a separate and distinct microcosm of connections within a social sphere that provides real-life issues individuals can work to solve (Perusse, Goodnough, & Lee, 2009). Chukhray discussed the density of the business marketplace to demonstrate the economy as dependent on the degree to which customers take advantage of the complex knowledge and resources, and synthesize the total information into decisions for individuals. Conyne and Cook (2004) discussed such interdependence while describing the unique ability of humans to "create structures around abstract ideas" (p. 7). Cooperation, collaboration, and competition for resources are ideas purported by Dutta and Sen (2003) as integral to the members' group functioning. The roles group members have outside of the group inherently follow them into the group setting as well (Strauss & U, 2007).

When the group leader attempts to influence the ecological (often external) factors, group performance is reported as enhanced (Wittenbaum et al., 2004). Ecological factors include, for example, the setting and social environment, the number of group participants, and whether the group is open or closed, mandated or voluntary. Laux, Smirnoff, Ritchie, and Cochrane (2007) identified pregroup screening as a necessity to assist in helping the person interact with the environment in the most beneficial ways, by informing potential group members of expectations, identifying the needs of potential members, and clarifying members' commitment to the purpose of the group. Assessment of the group's purpose is inherent in the formation of a group, including a type of plan.

The context of the proposed group determines many of the planning steps needed to achieve a successful outcome for the group leader and members. The degree to which the group's purpose is achieved often is determined by the extent of the planning process. The group plan includes important practical details about what space is needed, what materials are needed, what access to the setting will be available (including the potential for disabled members), and what time frame is desired and reasonable to achieve the group's goals, but it also provides information to encourage member participation and explain what financial obligations they will incur, as well as how these will be handled (Rapin & Keel, 1998, Sec. A.A.5).

Relational demography offers insight into how individuals and groups of people compare their specific characteristics (e.g., sex, race, age) with those of others in a work environment, at times creating undesired work consequences (Chattopadhyay, Tluchowska, & George, 2004; Valenti & Rockett, 2008). Although self-categorization theory assumes that individuals prefer to interact with members of their own social groups (Schmitt, Branscombe, Silvia, Garcia, & Spears, 2006), relational demography recognizes that workers are generally unable to select the people with whom they work, who may be persons of diverse backgrounds and experiences. Consequently, the demographic differences between individuals and among group members are likely to affect individual group members and the group itself.

In organizations, it is common to utilize group processes to work on tasks, since many individuals have pieces of information and specific expertise that, when brought together, offer a solution that combines their various knowledge (Mojzisch & Schulz-Hardt, 2010). Political agendas drive decisions about some groups that are created to assist in decision making. Similarly, reports on such groups include the same benefits that corporations have noted—mainly the potential exchange of knowledge and information, much of which is specialized depending on the organization to be represented within the group (Renou, 2011). In educational settings, educators are also likely to use groups to assist students in completing tasks and making decisions. Instructors, particularly, have come to realize that the students' perceptions of their groups begin with the group formation (Hilton & Phillips, 2010).

Regardless of group type (e.g., task, psychoeducational, counseling, therapy) or purpose (e.g., prevention, development, remediation, problem solving), a number of ecological and ethical factors affect the formation process. These include setting, organization rules and regulations, state or provincial laws and practice regulations, age of group members, limits of confidentiality in group work, managed care, group time limits, supervisor qualifications in group work, and member expectations of change. Group membership, including population served; how to locate, recruit, screen, and select participants; and how participants will benefit from the group also have impact on group outcomes. Leader training, scope of practice, and supervision arrangements dictate the range and variety of group activities to be implemented. Subsequent chapters will demonstrate each of these topics and include supporting literature.

Overview of Formation Steps

The following formation steps have been arbitrarily separated into discrete chapters because the formation decisions flow naturally from one step to the next. However, the same information is often used for more than one step. For example, information gathered about a potential group member may assist leaders in identifying the person as appropriate for group in the recruiting step, in assigning the individual to a specific group in the screening step, and in providing pregroup information in the selecting step. In each step, some roadblocks (e.g., setting, ethical issues) will be identified, along with planning process tools to minimize them. In addition, we have integrated material regarding multicultural considerations throughout the book. Multicultural perspectives and strategies, if well formulated and implemented, should form part of the web of the group plan and not be relegated to one step or another.

Organize

A number of important ecological considerations are determined in this step. Where is the group to be sponsored and conducted? Is it accessible to the identified group-participant population? If the group is intended for a rural community, potential side effects that are different from those in an urban setting must be considered. Is this a new venture? Is your group a part of an ongoing menu of groups? Do you have supervisory and administrative support for the group? What does the physical space look like, and can it be configured for maximum group benefit? Are there time limits for group session and group length? Are research or treatment protocols required? Is this a group with one leader or coleaders? If co-led, have you planned for your roles? Are your skills and styles compatible? Are you in compliance with any organization, state, or professional codes and statutes? Are you working with a student group leader?

Market and Recruit

Are you using a planning group? How does the sponsoring organization, be it independent practice, agency, school, inpatient setting, or community setting, relate to the community and its identified needs? What brand already exists for the sponsoring organization with regard to offering groups? Are you conducting an optional group or one with required attendance (e.g., court-ordered anger-management group)? How are you going to advertise the group? Are you working with managed-care organizations?

In recruiting members, other questions are relevant. What evidence exists for matching particular groups to populations? Are there specific ethical considerations in working with your population (e.g., children)? Do you take referrals from current or previous clients? How do you coordinate care within the organization? Are there therapeutic approaches that serve specific group populations? How might you exclude individuals from a group? How does your scope of practice influence recruitment?

Screen

What tools do you plan to use for screening potential members? Are you using standardized instruments? Are you interviewing? If so, what information will you gather and why? Are you screening people into or out of the group? What information would you need to do either? How will you use research to assist you in group member screening?

Select

In the member selection process, leaders use information from screening interviews and tools to answer the following questions: Who best matches the goals of the group? Who can contribute in a group setting? Who can model desirable group member behaviors? Who can contribute to collaborative learning and skill development? Who will be able to practice and demonstrate specific goal behaviors? Do permissions need to be secured for group member participation?

Compose

The final step ensures that leaders and members have the ultimate choice in becoming active participants in the group. What happens if you are working with an intact group? Can people opt out once the group has begun? How can a pregroup meeting assist you in this process? What items should be included in an orientation or pregroup meeting? Will the members be committed to a certain number of sessions? What should the members expect of leaders and themselves?

Theoretical and Conceptual Support

Ethics and training standards documents provide mandated and aspirational guidance to group leaders. There are, however, great variations in ethics documents across professions. Professional associations devoted specifically to group work have developed additional tools, including best practice guidelines, training standards, multicultural group work competencies, and practice guidelines for group therapy (Rapin, 2011). An overview of these counseling, psychology, and social work documents, and their similarities and differences, is presented here. In each of these professions, ethics guidelines tend to be general in nature and limit specific comments about group practice. When group practice is mentioned in ethics codes, it is highlighted to provide protection to group members and students in training. Integration of these ethics and best practices in the group formation step is essential to ethical and effective group practice.

Broad Counseling Documents

The American Counseling Association (ACA, 2005) restructured its ethics code to encompass minimum expected behaviors of all members of the association and eliminated the previously accompanying standards of practice document. Three areas of group practice are stipulated in counseling relationships: privileged communication, confidentiality and privacy, and supervision, training, and teaching.

Regarding the counseling relationship, ACA (2005) states,

> When a counselor agrees to provide counseling services to two or more persons who have a relationship, the counselor clarifies at the outset which person or persons are clients and the nature of the relationships the counselor will have with each involved person. If it becomes apparent that the counselor may be called upon to perform potentially conflicting roles, the counselor will clarify, adjust, or withdraw from roles appropriately. (p. 5)

Regarding screening, a formation step that will be detailed later in the book, ACA states,

> Counselors screen prospective group counseling/therapy participants. To the extent possible, counselors select members whose needs and goals are compatible with goals of the group, who will not impede the group process, and whose well-being will not be jeopardized by the group experience. (p. 5)

In considering protection of group participants, ACA (2005) states, "In a group setting, counselors take reasonable precautions to protect clients from physical, emotional, or psychological trauma" (p. 5). In considering the limits of confidentiality in group work, ACA states, "In group work, counselors clearly explain the importance and parameters of confidentiality for the specific group being entered" (p. 8). It also sets parameters around the definition of the "client" by stating,

In couples and family counseling, counselors clearly define who is considered "the client" and discuss expectations and limitations of confidentiality. Counselors seek agreement and document in writing such agreement among all involved parties having capacity to give consent concerning each individual's right to confidentiality and any obligation to preserve the confidentiality of information known. (p. 8)

In consideration of training and supervision relationships, ACA (2005) states,

Counselor educators make every effort to ensure that the rights of peers are not compromised when students or supervisees lead counseling groups or provide clinical supervision. Counselor educators take steps to ensure that students and supervisees understand they have the same ethical obligations as counselor educators, trainers, and supervisors. (p. 15)

Ethics references for additional counseling associations related to practice settings are notable. The American College Personnel Association (ACPA)–College Student Educators International represents many group practitioners in higher education settings—most typically in college and university counseling and mental health centers. The ACPA (2006) reference to group work practice states,

Assure that required experiences involving self-disclosure are communicated to prospective graduate students. When the preparation program offers experiences that emphasize self-disclosure or other relatively intimate or personal involvement (e.g., group or individual counseling or growth groups), professionals must not have current or anticipated administrative, supervisory, or evaluative authority over participants. (p. 4)

Those working in community mental health centers may very likely be members of the American Mental Health Counselors Association (AMHCA) and adhere to its code of ethics. AMHCA (2010) states, about confidentiality,

In working with families or groups, the rights to confidentiality of each member should be safeguarded. Mental health counselors must make clear that each member of the group has individual rights to confidentiality and that each member of a family, when seen individually, has individual rights to confidentiality within legal limits. (p. 3)

Regarding screening of group members, AMHCA states,

When working in groups, mental health counselors screen prospective group counseling/therapy participants. Every effort is made to select members whose needs and goals are compatible with goals of the group, who will not impede the group process, and whose well-being will not be jeopardized by the group experience. (p. 5)

AMHCA also states, "In the group setting, mental health counselors take reasonable precautions to protect clients from physical, emotional, and psychological harm or trauma" (p. 5).

The American School Counselor Association (2010) and its ethical standards further guide professional counselors in school settings. These standards include additional protections for minor children in group work. The entirety of Item A.6 pertains to group work. It states the following:

a. Screen prospective group members and maintain an awareness of participants' needs, appropriate fit and personal goals in relation to the group's intention and focus. The school counselor takes reasonable precautions to protect members from physical and psychological harm resulting from interaction within the group. (p. 3)

b. Recognize that best practice is to notify the parents/guardians of children participating in small groups.

c. Establish clear expectations in the group setting, and clearly state that confidentiality in group counseling cannot be guaranteed. Given the developmental and chronological ages of minors in schools, recognize the tenuous nature of confidentiality for minors renders some topics inappropriate for group work in a school setting.

d. Provide necessary follow up with group members, and document proceedings as appropriate.

e. Develop professional competencies, and maintain appropriate education, training and supervision in group facilitation and any topics specific to the group.

f. Facilitate group work that is brief and solution-focused, working with a variety of academic, career, college and personal/social issues. (p. 3)

The certification organization that governs many counselors, the National Board for Certified Counselors (2005), also has a code of ethics that includes group practice protections for participants. Section 1 states, "In a group setting, the certified counselor is also responsible for taking reasonable precautions to protect individuals from physical and/or psychological trauma resulting from interaction within the group" (p. 3). Further highlighting the complications in protecting group member confidentiality, Item 16 states,

In group counseling, counselors clearly define confidentiality . . . and discuss the difficulties related to confidentiality involved in group work. The fact that confidentiality cannot be guaranteed is clearly communicated to group members. However, counselors should give assurance about their professional responsibility to keep all group communications confidential. (p. 4)

Broad Social Work Document

Consistent with ethics documents in counseling, the National Association of Social Workers (2008) specifies confidentiality limits in group work:

> When social workers provide counseling services to families, couples, or groups, social workers should seek agreement among the parties involved concerning each individual's right to confidentiality and obligation to preserve the confidentiality of information shared by others. Social workers should inform participants in family, couples, or group counseling that social workers cannot guarantee that all participants will honor such agreements. (Sec. 1.07f)

Additionally, the code states, "Social workers should inform clients involved in family, couples, marital, or group counseling of the social worker's, employer's, and agency's policy concerning the social worker's disclosure of confidential information among the parties involved in the counseling" (Sec. 1.07g).

Broad Psychology Document

Psychology ethics documents published by the American Psychological Association (2002, 2010) identify leader responsibilities in groups and the protections required for student trainees in groups. Aside from these specific references, the psychology ethics code is general in nature. Item 10.03 governs the general practice of group psychology and states, "When psychologists provide services to several persons in a group setting, they describe at the outset the roles and responsibilities of all parties and the limits of confidentiality" (American Psychological Association, 2002, p. 14). Item 7.02, regarding training programs, states,

> Psychologists responsible for education and training programs take reasonable steps to ensure that there is a current and accurate description of the program content (including participation in required course- or program-related counseling, psychotherapy, experiential groups, consulting projects, or community service), training goals and objectives, stipends and benefits, and requirements that must be met for satisfactory completion of the program. This information must be made readily available to all interested parties. (p. 9)

Item 7.05 delineates responsibilities when group participation is mandatory, stating,

a. When individual or group therapy is a program or course requirement, psychologists responsible for that program allow students in undergraduate and graduate programs the option of selecting such therapy from practitioners unaffiliated with the program.

b. Faculty who are or are likely to be responsible for evaluating students' academic performance do not themselves provide that therapy. (American Psychological Association, 2002, p. 10)

Group Specialty Documents

Four group specialty associations—two from counseling, one from social work, and one interdisciplinary—serve as source examples for specific group resources. Each of the specialty documents noted here have direct application to the formation step in group work. Some of the specialty documents are aspirational in nature, which means that they cannot be interpreted as requirements for practice. The Association for Specialists in Group Work (ASGW), a division of ACA, has published aspirational best practice guidelines (Rapin & Keel, 1998; Thomas & Pender, 2008), training standards (Wilson, Rapin, & Haley-Banez, 2000), principles for diversity-competent group work (Haley-Banez et al., 1999), and social justice and multicultural group competencies (Singh, Merchant, Skudrzyk, & Ingene, 2012).

The Council for Accreditation of Counseling and Related Educational Programs (CACREP, 2009) has published program accreditation standards in which group work is one of eight required core areas for master's-level counselors. The Association for the Advancement of Social Work with Groups (AASWG) is affiliated with national social work associations in the United States and Canada and has published aspirational standards for the practice of social work with groups (AASWG, 2005). The American Group Psychotherapy Association (AGPA) is an interdisciplinary association whose members follow the ethics of their parent organizations. AGPA published aspirational clinical practice guidelines for group psychotherapy (Bernard et al., 2008) and, with the National Registry of Certified Group Psychotherapists (2002), certification guidelines for ethics.

Rapin (2011) conducted a review and comparison of current best practice guidelines and training standards from counseling, social work, and psychology. Rapin found that the training standards documents varied on target audience (master's, doctoral, terminal, licensed), competencies covered (core and/or advanced), group types specified (none, task or psychoeducational, counseling or therapy, therapy), and number of courses and/or clock hours required. CACREP standards have no specific number of courses required in group theory, knowledge, and skills but require coverage in five general areas: group dynamics, leadership or facilitation styles, theories of group counseling, group counseling methods, and group experience in counseling curricula. CACREP requires 10 hours of group experience in one academic term. ASGW has both master's-level and doctoral-level standards, with core areas for master's students gained in one course and 10 required hours of observation and participation, and 20 recommended hours. For doctoral or specialty levels, ASGW has advanced requirements for task and psychoeducational groups, with 30 hours of additional required training and 45 hours recommended, and for counseling or therapy groups, 45 hours of additional specialty training and 60 hours recommended. AGPA issues Certified Group Therapist credentials to professionals with terminal specialty degrees and advanced competencies, and requires 300 hours in group leading and 75 hours of supervision.

In comparing best practice documents across counseling, social work, psychology, and interdisciplinary groups, Rapin (2011) found consistency in areas of critical importance to group leaders. Consistencies that apply to the group formation step are highlighted.

ASGW's best practices in planning include (a) professional context and regulatory requirements, (b) scope of practice and professional framework, (c) assessment, (d) program development and evaluation, (e) resource coordination, (f) professional disclosure statement, (g) group and member preparation, (h) professional development, and (i) integration of trends and technological advances (Rapin & Keel, 1998; Thomas & Pender, 2008).

AASWG (2005) describes a pregroup phase including planning, recruitment, and new group formation. Identified are 15 group tasks and skills, including (a) needs assessment of potential members, (b) organization support, (c) recruitment, (d) group member preparation, and (e) consideration of potential contextual, environmental, and societal impacts on the group. Fifteen required knowledge competencies are also identified, including (a) organization mission and influence on the nature and development of group work service, (b) influence of cultural factors on potential members' lives, (c) issues associated with group structure, and (d) contracting procedures. These best practices are incorporated in the formation steps to follow.

Sequential steps organize the AGPA best practice document (Bernard et al., 2008). Steps in the formation stage include (a) creating successful therapy groups, client referrals, and administrative collaboration; (b) therapeutic factors and mechanisms; (c) member selection, premature termination, and selection instruments; (d) therapy group composition; and (e) preparation and pregroup training. The document mandates that the group leader integrate knowledge of variables that include the population served, individual member interpersonal characteristics, state-of-the-group development, timing of appropriate interventions, and dynamic whole-group factors. In providing support to clinical practitioners, this document also emphasizes appropriate group membership through the leader's referral sources. Providing full disclosure on the intent of the group, the purpose, and all planning details helps the referral process include potential members that are well suited to the specific group being formed (Bernard et al., 2008).

Barlow (2012) applied a group competency model to demonstrate psychology group-specialty practice. Barlow presented a series of flow charts delineating (a) group types originating from group dynamics, (b) pregroup assessment, and (c) postgroup assessment. Barlow identified foundational competencies, shared by all psychology specialties, and applied them to group practice. Barlow also delineated cross-professional functional group competencies for entry-level group psychologists, including knowledge-based competencies and applied competencies in assessment, interventions, consultation, research, supervision and training, and management and administration—broadly applicable to psychology, counseling, and social work group practice.

Learning Exercise

Background for Developing a Group

The purpose of this exercise is to gain some practice in developing a group and using valuable resources to do so.

1. In small groups of no more than three people, obtain access to the multiple group documents that inform best practices, as identified in this chapter.

2. Identify all appropriate documents that are applicable to each question.

3. Answer the following questions:

   a. Which document specifically addresses doctoral-level training standards?

   b. Where would you locate ethics competencies for group work?

   c. Where does a supervisor go to understand the training needs of students in counseling, social work, and psychology?

   d. Which documents cover details of group formation, such as screening and group member selection?

2 Organize

Many groups fail because leaders miss critical substeps in the organizing phase. While planning cannot eliminate all problems, it can remove some obstacles to success. Elements of organization include many of the basic planning steps, such as obtaining a space, collecting materials and resources, and more, which are covered in this chapter.

Professional Context and Regulatory Requirements

It may seem superfluous to formally consider the requirements of practice in your setting (American Psychological Association [APA], 2010; American School Counselor Association, 2010; Association for the Advancement of Social Work with Groups [AASWG], 2005; Thomas & Pender, 2008), but doing so will highlight setting-specific requirements. For example, if you work in a setting that limits treatment to short-term interventions, then the group plan you have formulated will need to comply with that treatment philosophy. If you are part of an interdisciplinary team, then you need to be aware of license requirements for each discipline and when these requirements conflict. These items become important especially when there are differences in profession or status among members of a work team. If the supervisor has a different license than the group leader or you and your coleader have different disciplines (psychologist and counselor, or professional and trainee, for example), issues of compliance become critical. Ohio serves as an example to demonstrate consistencies and differences in statutes that affect group planning. In Ohio, one set of laws and regulations governs counselors and social workers and another set governs psychologists and school psychologists. While it is a good idea to have a written scope of practice (see Thomas & Pender, 2008), Ohio counselors and social workers are required by statute to provide and post a written scope of practice in their work setting. Psychologists and school psychologists have no such requirement. In this example, interdisciplinary teams would follow the higher requirement.

Prior to the more concrete items, organizing may be done significantly in advance of other planning tasks if, for example, group leaders intend to conduct research. Obtaining institutional approval within the research standards as set forth by governmental and other institutional review boards may require lead time preceding other initial organizational tasks. You need to be aware of the review board meeting schedule and plan for potential modifications to your research design. Once research approval is obtained, then facility permissions may also require some degree of time lag prior to the anticipated start of the group. Some specific facility-based training may be expected of group leaders to uphold a sponsor's or corporate brand.

Resources

It is helpful to conduct a resource inventory during the formation step (Rapin & Keel, 1998; Thomas & Pender, 2008). At this time, you can identify what resources you will need to accomplish your group goals. You have the opportunity to define in advance if there are key decision makers who may influence the success or failure of your group (American Group Psychotherapy Association [AGPA], 2007a). You can determine if a planning group is appropriate and who might be helpful at each stage of development. If you budget time required to accomplish substeps in this planning phase, you will possibly avoid one of the most frequent errors in planning: setting an arbitrary time frame for planning and then finding it insufficient to complete all the planning activities. It is much better to take the additional time up front, acknowledging that it does indeed take more time to plan well, than to suffer the consequences of an inferior formation plan.

Time

One way to consider the tasks of organizing resources is around the dimension of time (Shulman, 2010). Consider group frequency and duration with the environment in mind. When working in an organization setting, match the group schedule and length of sessions to the availability of potential members. In educational settings, for example, successful groups parallel class time or after-school activities. This consideration would apply in slightly different fashion in comparing elementary school hours and class length, and middle and high school schedules. For example, Clarke, Lewinsohn, and Hops (2000) described a psychoeducation group for adolescents with depression that consisted of 16 two-hour sessions as an after-school activity over an eight-week period. They demonstrated that planning around the school calendar provided more potential member matches. It is easy to miss scheduled days off, special events, and religious holidays if specific organization information is not consulted. In community settings, it may be necessary to schedule groups in the late afternoon or early evening to maximize attendance and reduce work-related or school schedule conflicts of members.

Planning and development activities often require more time than desired or anticipated. The long-term investment in relationship building within and among agencies supports strong programs. To have a vibrant group program, time must be budgeted.

The Six Ms

Another model for considering necessary resources includes assessment of management support, manpower, materials, methods, machines, and money—broadly conceived. In many cases, consideration of one resource has impact on the others. It is wise to have an understanding of resource costs from various perspectives. Staff costs include scheduled group time, planning and between-group meetings (Thomas & Pender, 2008), supervision costs, and record-keeping costs for individual and group records.

Management Support

If you are working in an organization setting, you may or may not have independence in providing group services. There are a number of questions to be answered in determining management support. A flow chart can be constructed to identify which questions apply to your situation and what steps can be taken to respond to these needs. Does the mission of the organization include the provision of group services at all? If yes, then you can proceed to the next item. If group service is endorsed, is it a major or ancillary service? For example, if the main therapeutic intervention is individual therapy/counseling complemented by group therapy, you need both to be informed by your organization's process for matching individuals to groups and to inform the organization of the new offering. Does the content of your group plan match community needs sufficient to fill a group (AASWG, 2005; AGPA, 2007a)? Will the group be a one-time offering or part of ongoing services?

Consistent with the organization mission, the group service has to match the needs of the population to be served. If you are very invested in providing a particular group, you may inadvertently experience wishful thinking about the readiness of the community to respond to the offering or about the level of interest in the group. Here is a real example:

A university counseling center was adding to its large array of group offerings by identifying underserved pockets of students. Among this group were dual-career-preparation couples. A staff team developed an impressive group program for this audience and had great success in filling the initial group. A research design was incorporated into the group plan. Of note was that the staff team members were all themselves in dual-career relationships and, as a collective, were greatly invested in the group. When it was time to offer the second round of the group, the counseling center had difficulty in identifying appropriate participants. The program development team assessed that while the dual-career content had merit, the group was taking up too much staff time and energy to sustain in its original design. The mainly undergraduate university simply had too few students who were appropriate for the group. The decision was made that the dual-career group could be only an occasional offering rather than one conducted during each term of the academic year.

Another question area has to do with how groups are filled (AASWG, 2005; AGPA, 2007a, 2007b). While we will discuss this issue in later chapters on marketing and recruiting, it is helpful to consider the overall work philosophy of the organization (from individual practice to large organization) and where groups fit in. Do your colleagues share an interest in groups? When potential clients interact with the intake staff of the organization, ensure that they are informed about the possibility for group treatment. Individual agency staff members may make group referrals. If so, referring staff are likely to experience negative side effects in their own billable units of service. For example, many agencies require a certain service delivery quotient from every staff member. When a staff member makes the decision to refer an individual client to group, the referring staff person has to take on a new client to maintain service quota. In situations where it is appropriate to continue individual counseling and add group treatment, the agency may consider the multiple interventions as inefficient.

If you are offering a new group service, ensure that it fits with or complements the treatment model(s) of the organization. You may have to educate the management and your colleagues about the advantages of group before you acquire tangible support. If so, you need to provide information that supports your group intervention(s) (Barlow, 2012; Burlingame, Fuhriman, & Mosier, 2003). If you are working in a managed-care environment, it may be that reimbursement rates and efficiencies of serving clients in groups, rather than appropriateness of treatment, are the driving sources of support (Acuff et al., 1999; Thomas & Pender, 2008). For example, if there is a long waiting list, clients may be directed to group services as a means of handling service volume, independent of group fit. Challenges in individual group practice affect income. If you are working in independent practice, you will need to determine if you have a sufficient client base to source your group(s). Insurance contracts do reimburse group treatment but at a lower rate than for individual service. To manage a group practice, you will have to calculate how many clients would need to be in your groups to maintain your practice. If you are in independent practice, you will need to have multiple strategies to gain access to potential members. Identify the informal managers in the community who will provide support for your group. Any of these questions relevant to your setting may require proactive work on your part, and time needs to be built into your program planning to ensure this fundamental support. This topic is further discussed in the marketing and recruiting chapter.

Manpower

In addition to administrative support, there are other manpower sources to consider. Central is the decision to use one leader or coleaders (Riva, Wachtel, & Lasky, 2004; Wilson, Rapin, & Haley-Banez, 2000). There are advantages and disadvantages to both models. Practical and sometimes nontherapeutic variables determine use of one leader or coleaders. Limits of staff time may dictate that only one person be assigned to lead any group, perhaps promoting efficiency. Coleaders may provide increased attention to content and process variables, thereby promoting effectiveness. Coleadership is likely to require more staff time and coordination in pregroup and between-group processing. Coleadership can also be used by the organization to provide backup protection if one leader is absent. If the coleader is in a training mode, sufficient resources need to be devoted to ongoing professional development of general and group-specific skills, as well as direct supervision and feedback to the sponsoring academic program (American Counseling Association [ACA], 2005; APA, 2010; Wilson et al., 2000). Senior leaders and their coleaders are held to the same professional standards and regulatory requirements (ACA, 2005; APA, 2010), so it is imperative that the coleader receives appropriate and consistent supervision (Riva, 2006).

Another manpower issue has to do with potential involvement of members of the client/community base in the planning for group services (AASWG, 2005; AGPA, 2007a). If your employer organization has a community board, relationships with other organizations (e.g., the courts, schools, churches, community agencies), or a training relationship with a university, we recommend that you build on the natural access your organization has to those resources. These outside relationships may assist in conducting needs assessments, providing support for particular group offerings, marketing, and member recruiting.

Materials

Physical location in the community or organization may affect potential members' interest in participation. Many community organizations have physical space not configured to support group work, and often there is no dedicated group space. Leaders have to consider and maximize positive dynamics in the group's environmental setting.

The ecological concepts of synomorphy—the nature of the fit between the occupants and the setting, interpersonal zones, and seating patterns—are relevant here. In his discussion of research on group spaces, Forsyth (2010) highlighted several physical elements that have potential effects on group members. For example, in many education settings, from elementary school through college and university level, classrooms are designed to direct attention from students to teacher. In many instances, chairs or desks are bolted to the floor in rows facing in one direction (toward the head of the class). The nature of participant interactions is sometimes secondary to the efficiency of the physical layout.

In our university experience, a long-awaited remodeling of classroom and hall space used by a counseling program and other programs was found to inhibit group participation. In one seminar/group room, long tables were arranged in a U shape but were bolted to each other and to the floor so that the furniture could not be reconfigured for the group classes, demonstrations, and group projects assigned to the space. In a nearby room, comfortable, movable seating shared space with a bank of drink machines, thereby inhibiting close conversation. In the hall, lockers were replaced with occasional small benches that did not promote conversation. Almost immediately, students and faculty identified the space and use mismatches. Rather than constructing sociopetal spaces to promote interaction, the project had the negative side effect of being sociofugal, inhibiting group communication. The finished wing looked beautiful but did not function well for its intended participants. Shortly after the remodel, an unidentified user of the space removed all the hardware securing the tables to the floor.

Seating arrangements also affect participation. In the above university example, the remodeled rooms were equipped with comfortable, adjustable swivel chairs. Until the stealth detachment of table-to-floor hardware, the chairs could not be reconfigured. Forsyth (2010) summarized that (a) circles are more likely to foster confinement and interpersonal attraction; (b) L-shaped groups foster more fidgeting and pauses in discussion; (c) circle seating is more positive for females than for males; (d) men favor sitting opposite from those they like and next to strangers; and (e) the reverse holds true for women, who prefer adjacent seating for those they like and opposite seating from strangers. Forsyth concluded, "Clearly, group members should be sensitive to the possibility that their spatial behaviors will be misinterpreted by others, and should be willing to make certain that any possible misunderstandings will be short-lived" (p. 461).

Printed materials, including leader materials, professional disclosure statements, screening and selection instruments, research instruments, member handouts, and evaluation tools, need to be anticipated, budgeted, and prepared (Rapin & Conyne, 2006). We have heard many tales of leaders frantically copying group materials right before the start of a group session. Take the time to assemble all you can during planning. Remember, you may have to modify some materials because of between-session debriefing and planning. Specialty materials—for example, video clips, playback machines, video screens, and biofeedback tools—need to be arranged in advance and should match the physical setting.

Client records, including their format, storage, and implementation, are guided by institutional rules (Zur, 2013), professional ethics (e.g., AASWG,

2005; ACA, 2005; AGPA, 2007a, 2007b; American College Personnel Association, 2006; APA, 2010; Thomas & Pender, 2008), federal law (e.g., Health Insurance Portability and Accountability Act), and state law (see Ohio Revised Code, Chapter 4732.07). Knauss (2006) identified key issues in record keeping and suggested that two sets of records be maintained for groups—one for each member of the group and one for general group progress toward goals.

Methods and Machines

Your group plan outlines activities you will employ. Theoretical methods and activities to demonstrate them should be coordinated (AASWG, 2005). If you are planning group activities that require movement, you need to ensure that you can adjust seating and return the room to the pregroup arrangement at the end of your session. You can easily incorporate this housekeeping activity into your member orientation. Record-keeping strategies (AGPA, 2007a; Price & Price, 1999) and consistency are essential for tracking effective and appropriate referrals.

Intentional building of relationships between group providers and administrators within organizations promotes long-term viability of group treatments. The AGPA (2007a, 2007b) practice guidelines for group therapy recommend the development of group coordinator positions in organizations with sufficient groups to support them. AGPA (2007a) and the Association for Specialists in Group Work (Thomas & Pender, 2008) recommend formal relationship building with managed-care companies. The intake staffs at managed-care companies are often the ones who recommend providers and also determine whether a particular treatment is reimbursable. Summarizing the worth of such relationship building, AGPA (2007a) states, "While this additional step further complicates and may delay the initial creation of therapy groups, there is little doubt that a collaborative relationship is essential in developing and sustaining psychotherapy groups" (p. 2).

Bernard et al. (2008) recommended methods for obtaining informed consent regarding intake forms and client records in group practice. She summarized benefits to the group practitioner and to group members, including increased accountability for the group practitioner, support for the group members' autonomy, shared ownership of treatment between the group leader and members, and increased visibility of treatment and termination goals.

Ongoing group research is essential to maintain high standards and best practices. In the event that the group leader chooses to evaluate any aspect of the group's process and performance, planning is involved. Various types of evaluation may be considered, from a qualitative observation procedure to skills-training exercises with self-report feedback and/or group member feedback to satisfaction surveys. Johnson and Johnson (2003) conceive of evaluation as evidence about desired outcomes and the perceptions of how well the outcomes were achieved. For example, in a qualitative observation data collection, the leader or assigned observer notes occurrences and reoccurrences of a particular behavior positively or negatively influencing the group process. In the case of skills training, the leader may ask group members to role-play and give feedback about how many times someone avoided asking questions in a reflective listening exercise. Though simple, these examples could be data collected over time, and overall satisfaction reports from each group member give the leader feedback about what did and did not work.

In any case, evaluation must have a clear purpose that includes methods of capturing data and how the data will be used. Yalom (2005) describes numerous examples of groups that have been used in research, emphasizing the importance of the rationale behind preparation. Additionally, informed consent involves further discussion with group members and often written notification for group members to concede to their participation in a group that is involved in research or in which they may be asked to give feedback to others. Group leaders often find it valuable to obtain member feedback as they are developing their skills and competencies. Similarly, formative evaluation along the way provides valuable information that could alter processes to most effectively achieve the goals from the group members' perspectives.

Money

It is important to consider the financial realities of group work and to determine how understanding costs of service can support your practice. If you work in an agency or large organization, you may not have to interact with clients about the cost of treatment, because finances are handled independently from treatment. In practical terms, however, it is important to have an understanding of client payment arrangements (e.g., self-pay, managed-care contracts, sliding scale) and equally important to understand how you are paid for group services. Individual practitioners are more likely to have firsthand experience deciding whether to offer a particular intervention as a group or individual service and more likely to experience the monetary consequences of their choices. In many cases, client flow and comfort/discomfort with group approaches determine group treatment, rather than the efficacy and appropriateness of group (Barlow, 2012).

Ethics

MacNair-Semands (2007) presented several perspectives on the ethical mandate to include not only consideration for the diversity of the group population and context but also the group leader's self-awareness of cultural bias. Rapin (2004) emphasized the uniqueness of each group member and group leaders. Social power is continually influential as individuals interact with others and with settings, whereby a group leader is responsible for processing how values, biases, cultures, or communities weave together. The impact of this open stance and attitude can be demonstrated in all ethical considerations of forming a group.

The group leader considers risks and benefits for the group's members, and thereafter must pay attention to the setting, or the environment in which the group will function. *For example, a community agency has requested a sequence of group meetings for psychoeducational purposes for three neighborhoods that interact within the school system. The director of the agency has offered a meeting hall that has been in use for more than 34 years. Though it is standing, there are serious plumbing and electrical code violations that could pose problems for anyone using the facility. What does the leader do in this case? The purpose of the group is admirable, links school and community, offers prevention and remediation activities and learning, and creates advocacy for enhanced communication with community leaders. Is there a potential ethical concern with talking to parents and families in a space that is relatively unsafe?*

An overarching concern of all group leaders and group members involves the issue of confidentiality limits (Corey, Corey, & Corey, 2010; Crowell, Sebera, & Coaston, 2012; Lasky & Riva, 2006; MacNair-Semands, 2007; Page, 2004; Rapin, 2004, 2013). Disclosure by a group member is not protected by the requirements of confidentiality as it is with the group leader. Posthuma (2002) addressed the leader's limitation to avoid any guarantee that group members will not disclose any information provided by others. Innocent disclosure can reveal the fact that two people know each other because they are in the same treatment group, or group leaders may disclose preauthorization information to an insurance company. Rapin (2004) reminds group leaders that national data banks have access to client information through insurance filing and managed-care communication.

Technology advances the information available to both group leaders and members, possibly assists in marketing a group, allows for easy assessment, and aids in other tasks—but not without consequences. Confidentiality concerns arise quickly when distance counseling is an option, for either individual or group interaction (Page, 2004). The culture of the Internet is without concerns for privacy and minimization of risks. This understanding is important in conceptualizing how therapeutic group work can be effective online. Even task groups or psychoeducational groups create opportunities for members to disclose personal information, which is potentially less secure over the Internet. However, this is not to say that online groups lack possible benefits.

Scope of Practice

Credentials for group leaders vary significantly depending on the type of group, population to be served, setting, professional standards, and more.

The APA (2002), ACA (1999), and National Board for Certified Counselors (2005) provide guidelines. A group leader's competency is measured by his or her ability to provide a dynamic and meaningful experience for group members based on the group's purpose and plan, performed within the limits of his or her scope of practice, and monitored for collaborative adjustments as needed. We have seen that there are documents under which various professionals practice to their profession's best standards and codes of ethics that guide professionals in their practice, but intragroup processing also informs the leader's practices. Despite a leader's professional competency level, the evaluation by the group's members and leader together is an imperative in processing (Bemak & Conyne, 2004).

Professional identity for group leaders is to be addressed in all professional reflective activities to ensure that their role is clear to themselves and to group members. Bemak and Conyne (2004) contended that a perspective of awareness of differing worldviews enables group leaders to better contextualize the influences of factors impacting what happens in group work. A framework is needed from which to develop the group plan and practices of performing and processing.

Theoretical orientation is considerably influential in leaders' choices about all aspects of planning, performing, and processing. *For example, a group will be open to voluntary members who are parenting school-aged children in two elementary and middle schools in one city. The parents have concerns following two recent gang-related fights in the community and will learn about choice theory in parenting. The leader will handle planning with tools that emphasize teaching basic concepts about how to understand total behavior (Wubbolding, 2000). In this instance,* choice theory *is the term identified for use with all interested learners, whereas* reality therapy *is the term used for counseling and psychotherapy. How the leader identifies professionally is important, since William Glasser Institute–certified people can teach choice theory but may not be able to practice counseling (reality therapy).*

Scope of practice with the identified client population is also a professional consideration for competent leadership. Just as in individual psychotherapy, where our goal is to assist the client in developing "a personal niche in which the individual can experience interpersonal effectiveness" (Wilson, 2004, p. 163), group leaders have the potential to help group members develop a group niche. In a homogeneous group of members of the same race and ethnicity, the same age group, or same gender, there is still significant variation among members. Sensitivity to the diversity of the population to be served is critical in the group leader's effectiveness performing and processing with the members. The ethical codes stress this point to facilitate group leaders' doing no harm.

Tang and Bashir (2012, p. 162) discussed cultural identity development as individuals seeking a sense of belonging in a multifaceted process. In our diverse society, it has become significantly important to understand how individual behavior depends a great deal on how the environment interacts with the individual's characteristics. When a person meets a new and different culture, self-awareness of his or her own cultural identity is heightened (Tang & Bashir, 2012). We all have a variety of identities, including cultural, religious, and sexual, and the unique combination of multiple facets means that they intersect and are interdependent. Comstock et al. (2008) stated that group leaders can acquire a variety of relational competencies to enable them to deal with "interpersonal and contextual dynamics" (p. 283) and help all group members collaborate on their perceptions of change. Groups, therefore, provide social events where individuals interact in an environment in which groups rarely isolate but, rather, coexist in a common society (Tang & Bashir, 2012).

One professional issue that may arise for a rural counseling setting is the possibility of repeated contact with group members outside of the group setting. When several leaders might be trained to lead a group to ensure continuity in case of illness or vacation, the potential pool of leaders may be reduced in a rural setting. Even when a leader works within an urban area, there may be a shortage of group leaders. For example, in a community that is rundown and noted for its crime statistics, available group leaders who are women may not desire to travel into certain neighborhoods at night for meetings, or group members may have the same perceptions of the lack of safety.

Supervision

For a high level of professionalism, group leaders access supervision regularly to process their work. Leaders have been influenced by their training, which includes their faculty and supervisors (Yager, 2004). Within supervision, group leaders have an opportunity to grow both personally and professionally to further enhance their group skills. A variety of instructional methods used in training for supervision also provides counselors with structures for processing silently on their own and then later in supervision sessions, such as in cognitive self-instruction (Yager, 2004). Whatever models the supervisor and group leader use, the group leader can rely on the support of supervision to further develop and change. In ecological terms, the group leader's microsystem is impacted by the interdependent and collaborative nature of supportive supervision and new learning.

In an integrative health setting, such as a hospital or clinic, group leaders may be working with professionals from multiple disciplines. Nurses, social workers, doctors, residents, counselors, clerks, and clergy could potentially share group leadership. Sensitivity to the professional perspective from which each leader functions enhances the ability of each one to develop meaning-making about how an ecological framework expands the potential for growth for each person involved. Counselors, for one, have a particular set of skills that enable them to understand their group members and discover how some people are hindered in their communication and, hence, their interpersonal relationships (Hall & Yager, 2012). Similarly, while working with professionals from other disciplines, opportunities arise to demonstrate the therapeutic benefits of group work, possibly in addition to or even in lieu of medication regimens for some clients. *For example, Grandison, Pharwaha, and Dratcu (2009) described an inpatient communications group instituted in an acute male psychiatric ward with no group treatment history. The team used Yalom's (1983) model for inpatient group therapy for a heterogeneous population to frame their goals and group structure. An initial core team of six facilitators and a clinical supervisor were drawn from a multidisciplinary team of psychiatry specialists, nurses, support workers, an occupational therapist, and the senior manager of the psychotherapy day service, all of whom had prior group experience. The program included a training model with more- and less-experienced facilitators and ongoing supervision.*

Learning Exercise

Write Your Personal Identity

From what you know at this point, write a description of yourself as (1) a group leader and (2) a group member. Your identity may be different in those two roles now that you have a great deal of awareness of the expectations and responsibilities. Consider your skills and strengths, and create an identity that could serve as an application to one of those roles in a group that is forming. Be creative in how you present yourself so that you use appropriate group work language that would ensure your obtaining the position.

3

Market Group and Recruit Members

_____ **Market**

While mental health marketing is generally challenging, marketing of group services can introduce additional factors that must be addressed. In many cases, the setting will determine the nature of marketing and recruiting (Berg, Landreth, & Fall, 2012). Shulman (2010) emphasized that group services are owned by the setting or organization in which they occur and not by the leader. Therefore, marketing of groups must be consistent with the goals of the organization setting. Marketing strategies may look very different when comparing the options of school-based groups with private-practice groups, or inpatient setting groups or court-mandated groups.

Planning Group

The planning group is useful for establishing and maintaining collaborative working relationships with referral sources, for educating the target population(s) in the scope and purposes of group offerings, to aid in defining essential elements of community needs, and to assist with ongoing program evaluation. Planning groups may include staff members, administrators, community members, or multiorganization groups. Strong working relationships are key to group program maintenance. In each setting, it is helpful to identify decision makers, potential referral sources, and sources of support or expertise. Some suggestions for planning group steps include the following:

- Define the goals of the planning group, which may be different from the specific group plan you will implement.
- Use the information you gathered in the organizing step about necessary resources to staff the planning group.
- Set milestones for the planning so that members know who is responsible for what tasks and time frames.
- Have clearly established roles for members.

- Remember to distinguish planning from execution. As the group leader, you are responsible for implementation.
- Debrief with any group evaluation data so that the planning group knows group plan adjustments.
- Use previous experience. The planning group may help you identify avoidable mistakes, recognize history of success with the type of group or group program to be implemented, compile fruitful referral sources, and share successful marketing and recruiting strategies.

Information from regional assessments of community needs can be used as initial data for planning offerings. For example, in the 20-county area in greater Cincinnati, Northern Kentucky, and Indiana, a number of group programs and collaborative groups have received funding for mental health efforts (Health Foundation of Greater Cincinnati, 2013). Aligning with such a resource can assist in targeting community needs, providing continuity of services across organization settings, and obtaining funding for worthy interventions.

In schools, strong relationships between school counselors and teachers, parents, administrators, and the larger community are important to successful groups. Community mental health agencies often provide services in schools to complement school-funded school counseling and school psychology services. School personnel and agency staff have the opportunity to extend their resources for group services in collaborating. Such collaboration of efforts can result in consensus on the service and support for groups (Shulman, 2010), among other gains.

Marketing to Managed Care

Managed-care companies are known for emphasizing efficiency, cost, and effectiveness of mental health services (Spitz, 1996). Evidence-based group treatments were sparse when Spitz (1996) wrote about group psychotherapy and managed mental health care. Now, with a focus on researching evidence-based care (Burlingame, Kapetanovic, & Ross, 2005), providers of group treatment are more likely to demonstrate the efficacy of group treatments, as well as their cost efficiency. Spitz described similarities between brief individual therapy and group therapy to demonstrate the benefits of group work within the managed-care business and practice climate. These include the following:

a. Screening before group to identify the individual's match with a particular group content and to rule out those who might not profit from an active approach. Managed-care companies generally require detailed information about the client (often a five-axis diagnosis), the presenting concerns, and coping strategies. These requirements have become more consistent with best practice models of care since managed care emerged in the 1980s.

b. Homogeneous matching of the potential member to the appropriate group for shared factors "in symptoms, problem sets, and other factors that promote rapid member-to-member identification and quicker group cohesiveness" (Spitz, 1996, p. 26).

c. Clarity of group goals and focus: "The emotional intensity dictated by the constraints of time are mitigated by the fact that the experience is time-limited for the group leader, thereby making him/her less vulnerable to 'burn out,' which can come from leading one or many intensive groups with difficult patient populations over long periods of time" (p. 27).

Now, group treatments are not limited to brief groups. For example, Tricare (2012), which insures military personnel, contracts with Humana Military in one region of the country to allow 60 group therapy sessions and 15 family therapy sessions for substance use disorders per every 365-day benefit period, with preauthorization required.

Managed-care insurance companies can assist with referrals in several ways. First, insurance subscribers can contact their insurance companies for provider referrals. Providers who participate on any managed-care panel must complete a practice information profile as part of contracting. The more detail providers can submit for publication by managed-care companies, the more exposure they will receive. Managed-care checklists include degree, licensure, ethnicity, languages, populations served, therapeutic approaches, and specialty content areas. Practice information is generally available online to all group subscribers. Managed-care companies use gatekeeping services, either with their own behavioral health intake staff or through a behavioral health care vendor. Taking the time to build a relationship with the gatekeepers can lead to appropriate group referrals, particularly in regions with a shortage of specialty providers. Organizations and individuals who specialize in group services can establish working relationships with managed-care companies. In any insurance market, local panel members can serve on managed-care committees and as information sources for the benefits of group counseling, group therapy, or support groups, all of which are covered mental health services. Professional organizations that establish relationships with managed-care companies can influence the public materials about group interventions. For example, ValueOptions (2012), a major managed-care company that contracts behavioral health services, uses for its group therapy information a publication authored by the American Group Psychotherapy Association.

Site-Specific Variables

The setting may have characteristics that either support or limit the success of group interventions. These ecological factors may be reflected in the mission of the organization and purposes for group. For example, there is conflicting information about the effectiveness of group interventions with college students. Krogel, Beecher, Presnell, Burlingame, and Simonsen (2009) suggest that group may not be as appropriate as individual treatment for college students because of demands and lifestyle, for example. Daner (2009), however, described a successful university counseling center approach (mission, orientation) with group as the primary treatment mode. These conflicting results may reflect a treatment bias among organization members, which transfers to potential group members—with one result seeing individual treatment as primary and targeted groups as complements and the other seeing group treatments as primary with individual therapy complements.

Recruit

Merely constructing a group plan is insufficient in obtaining the group members. Once your marketing attempts have provided information to potential group participants, you will want to find people who will benefit from the group and even add to the group process. Publicity is just one step in informing the community that a group will exist, as members can also gain awareness from professional referrals by colleagues, community announcements or newsletters, and professional organizations' communication networks. Corey, Corey, and Corey (2010) stated that personal contact is desirable over commercializing an invitation to join.

What evidence is there about the right people for different types of groups? It is essential that the group's goals are compatible with the members' goals. Information is critical in the various forms of publicity used to attract the right people. Gladding (2008) suggested an information statement with descriptions of the group purpose and possible activities, as well as expectations of group members. The more information provided to potential members, the more the potential members will do some amount of self-screening. To suggest that there are right people for specific types of groups depends on many factors.

Johnson and Johnson (2003) explore group goals extensively. The focus on some shared vision by group members is an ideal and, when shared, clarifies the group's mission and purpose. Lewin (as cited in Johnson & Johnson, 2003) stated that group members could maximize both individual outcomes and goals through attention to the shared or joint outcomes. People who can commit to the group goals are more likely to be right for the group.

The quality of relationships is a necessity (Johnson & Johnson, 2003) for interpersonal communication and interactions. The conceptual underpinnings identified by Conyne (1999) demonstrate the value leaders hold for group work and its potential for meaningful change. Best practices, core competencies, and ethics guide the group leader's behaviors. A conceptual framework also needs to be communicated to group members so that the right people recognize the relational potential of the group, understand the leader's qualifications, anticipate evaluation methods, and commit to the group methods, strategies, activities, and techniques (Conyne, Crowell, & Newmeyer, 2008). Diversity is a key element in relationship quality, highlighting the importance of sensitivity to culture, race, ethnicity, ableism, and more.

Referrals

Referrals are an important source for your group members, emphasizing the value of professional networking among the helping professions. Colleagues may be working with individuals who would benefit from the interaction of group counseling or the psychoeducation that may be the focus of your group plan. Another potential referral source is your own current or former clients. Specific considerations need to be dealt with for any of these options. If a colleague refers an individual to you, one question that might arise is whether that colleague expects some type of feedback. Similarly, if a client refers someone, there may be an expectation that even casual conversation could include "how my friend is doing." In each of these cases, whether the group is psychoeducational or counseling in focus, the group members are entitled to privacy. Counselors are ethically required to maintain that confidentiality, which draws a line—a boundary between colleagues and clients and the group leader. The ethical group leader would take the time to educate referral sources to the leader's confidentiality requirement, thereby enhancing the likelihood that the boundary remain acceptable to the other party and preserve the relationship. The American Group Psychotherapy Association (2007a) reminds group leaders, and particularly private-practice members, to use their colleagues as referral sources and to cultivate colleagues' knowledge base about the advantages of group.

An interesting dilemma is when a new leader inherits an intact group. How does a leader continue what has been sold by another professional? Recruitment is an aspect of public relations during which the group members are courted to some degree (Gladding, 2008). Once engaged, group members need to be supported in their choice to participate. The group leader must be aware of what was included in the recruitment of the intact group membership and either continue to encourage participation with the awareness that some transition will happen with leader style, skills, and personality, or negotiate changes, recognizing that some group members may disengage.

Recruiting Minors

Gladding (2008) and Delucia-Waack (2006) emphasized the ethical and legal responsibilities involved when the group will consist of minors. First steps often include information provided to the minors, with follow-up information provided to parents or guardians. Assent is sought from the minor, while parental consent is needed to fulfill the professional ethics mandate. Clear and specific confidentiality discussion must occur to promote effective group functioning, as well as the minor's sense of safety and empowerment to participate fully. The creation of a caring environment is the foundation for the development of a social system in the group that will support member commitment, effective collaboration, sense of integrity among members and the leader, quality interconnection, and sustainability (Conyne et al., 2008). Screening will be an important step to seek participants who will benefit and to avoid individuals' being harmed by a group.

Learning Exercise

Recruitment Presentation

Create a PowerPoint presentation for recruiting group members to your young adult group (ages 19–24), which will run for a specified period of time (you choose the time span). It is a psychoeducation group with a topic of focus (you choose the topic). Utilize the information from this chapter to assist you in developing a well-thought-out recruitment media piece to use in a community setting (you choose the setting).

4

Screen

Screening and member selection are intertwined in several ways—for example, in their use of information gained from the same source (as with screening and selection instruments), use of interviews, and pregroup preparation. Therefore, these two formation steps will reference similar research. For information beyond the scope of this chapter, see Book 7, by Maria T. Riva and Robin Lange, in this series.

Forsyth (2010) reviewed a number of group dynamics internal and external to the individual that affect the operation in any group. For example, the need for affiliation helps determine what types of groups are attractive to any individual. According to social comparison theory, people respond to ambiguous situations in predictable ways. Forsyth identified a two-dimensional model of attachment style that may predict how people respond to joining a group. The four conditions are preoccupied (high anxiety and low avoidance), fearful (high anxiety and high avoidance), secure (low anxiety and low avoidance), and dismissing (high avoidance and low anxiety). Forsyth reported on Schachter's (1959) research on affiliation to describe the need to join with others facing similar situations ("misery loves company"; p. 96), the need to share useful information ("misery loves miserable company"; p. 97), and the need to avoid joining a group if it risks embarrassment ("embarrassed misery avoids company"; p. 97).

Gans and Counselman (2010) noted that culture also influences the group members' experiences. Since some individuals report strong affiliations to their culture, race, or ethnicity, screening requires sensitivity on the part of the counselor, to avoid a "one-size-fits-all approach" (Yalom, 2005, p. 259). Similarly, Corey, Corey, and Corey (2010) encouraged diversity within groups, maintaining the emphasis on the type and topical nature of the group.

Association for Specialists in Group Work (Haley-Banez et al., 1999) approved principles for diversity-competent group workers to attend most fully to the issue of diversity in professional practice and training. In 2012, ASGW revised, expanded, and renamed the document to embrace multicultural and social justice competence principles (Singh, Merchant, Skudrzyk, & Ingene, 2012). ASGW states,

The current document uses the term multiculturalism to align with the most recent language used in multicultural counseling scholarship, which embraces a broader perspective of recognizing unique world-views, appreciating socio-cultural differences, and facilitating the empowerment of individuals within a society. (p. 313)

ASGW defines the term *social justice* as "influences of both privilege and oppression that shape the well-being of individuals, groups, and communities" (p. 313). Notable is that the field of social work has embraced social justice principles throughout its history and documents. Psychology has a loose affiliation of American Psychological Association divisions that have endorsed social justice principles, among them Group Psychology and Group Psychotherapy.

The group leader must develop a personal awareness of other cultures and self-awareness of racial identity and personal worldview (DeLucia-Waack, 2004). Sensitivity to questions in interviews would be important to develop based on these awarenesses and context of the group and populations being recruited.

In a 1997 national survey of ASGW members regarding group member selection methods, Riva, Lippert, and Tackett (2000) found that individual screening interviews were the most common tool (68%), client requests were second most used (65.3%), and then referral from another counselor (54.7%), mandated assignment (42.7%), personality assessment instrument (26.7%), assessment measure of interpersonal/group behavior (18.7%), and group format screening interview (10.7%). These data are important when considering which screening approach(es) you will use. If you use resources predating 2005, you most likely will find fewer references to strategies other than interviews than you will find in literature that is more recent.

The basis for a group plan begins with a general description of proposed group, by type of group and rationale for the group (Conyne, Crowell, & Newmeyer, 2008, p. 45). The counselor's role must be kept in mind, particularly as it relates to the context of the group and setting. The group's context may include a diverse population, a variety of client ages, and certainly a setting that might be in a school, a community agency, a religious location, or other venues. School settings require strict adherence to policy, timing, available participants, and oversight (Conyne et al., 2008). Therefore, interviews align with the same restrictions set forth within the group plan.

Yalom (2005) contends that group work is quite complex and yet all factors are interdependent and function as definable variables with combined benefits. The 11 primary therapeutic factors are as follows:

- Instillation of hope
- Universality
- Imparting information
- Altruism

- The corrective recapitulation of the primary family group
- Development of socializing techniques
- Imitative behavior
- Interpersonal learning
- Group cohesiveness
- Catharsis
- Existential factors

Keeping these factors in mind for the best group outcome, screening and selecting group members are sensitive processes. Always keep in mind that a consistent positive relationship between leaders and members will be the measure of effective outcomes.

Competent assessment of potential group members will be made manifest in the group and individual outcomes. Gans and Counselman (2010) stated that in general, "patients with no prior therapy experience do less well in group therapy than patients who have had . . . competently managed individual therapy" (p. 216). The therapeutic relationship begins with the screening process.

Role Play

A variety of methods may be used in screening. Role play is one option, in which the counselor describes a brief group scenario and invites the potential group member to create a response.

A brief example might be when the group leader presents to a potential member, Julianne, a scenario in which another group member remarked that she felt a strong reaction to Julianne's statements about getting frustrated with her elderly mother. In the scenario, the other group member, Maria, stated that she was shocked by Julianne's comment because, so far, Julianne had seemed so nice and what she said sounded unkind. The group leader then asks Julianne to create a response that she believes would be appropriate in the group in this situation. From the response, the counselor gathers meaningful data about Julianne's belief system and possible interactional behaviors.

Interviews

The most popular method of screening is interview (Riva et al., 2000). Interviews can be done individually or in groups. If an instrument is utilized, the leader can use the individual's responses to guide the interview. A standard set of interview questions may also be developed, as suggested by group specialists (Capuzzi, Gross, & Stauffer, 2010; Corey et al., 2010; Delucia-Waack, 2006; Gazda, 1989; Jacobs, Masson, & Harvill, 2009; Johnson

& Johnson, 2003; Yalom, 2005). Information considered pertinent to the interview includes "environmental stresses, personal history, and inferences about motivation for treatment and ego strength" (Yalom, 2005, p. 261). Another piece of information that would help the leader assess a potential member would be whether the choice for the group was a personal one or one imposed by others.

Components of Interviews

Questions for interviews will be determined by the group's purpose, goals, and context. Jacobs et al. (2009) listed questions that draw from the potential group member information they may already have about the group and, at the same time, the self-perception the member has about goodness of fit. Capuzzi et al. (2010) listed questions such as these:

Why do you want to be in the group?

What do you expect from being a part of the group?

What experience do you have being in groups?

What could you contribute to the group?

What questions do you have about the group or the group leader?

Other pertinent questions might be influenced by the group's population, where member differences are expected to be highly visible:

What concerns you about your ability to participate in the group?

What personality or attitudinal aspects of your other group members would keep you from participating fully in the group?

When would you feel comfortable or uncomfortable talking about differences among group members?

What are you aware of in yourself that would impede your ability to be open and honest in the group?

Gazda (1989) offered guidelines about what information to provide to the potential group member as well. His recommendations guided the potential member to do her or his own preparation before the group selection as a way of assessing personal commitment and motivation.

Direct Sampling of Relevant Behavior

Behavior sampling can be especially helpful in situations that require certain behaviors or conditions to be present for group participation. For example, in a hospital setting, it may be essential to compose groups of heterogeneous diagnoses but commonality on the ability to talk about symptoms or symptom reduction strategies. Observing patients in the hospital environment may give staff essential information for inclusion or exclusion. Coding systems requiring trained raters—for example, the Interaction Process Analysis (Bales, 1999)—can be used both in the screening process and in measuring improvement in key behaviors. Pregroup interviews, conducted in a group with potential group members, can provide a sampling of desired group behaviors. For example, Berg, Landreth, and Fall (2012) suggest that individual screening interviews are not always possible and that the first group meeting can be used as a sample of desired member behaviors. See the following section regarding observations in school settings.

Screening Minors

Several authors (Delucia-Waack, 2006; Hines & Fields, 2002; Nock & Kurtz, 2005) observe that school settings are particularly well suited to direct observation, and they suggest several coding systems that can be employed to measure key behaviors. Hines and Fields (2002) identified pregroup screening issues for school counselors. The authors identified advantages school counselors have in their normal work environments to observe students over time and make informed decisions on group composition based on age, developmental level, gender, and diversity issues. They developed a pregroup screening protocol and matrix that school counselors and others doing group work in school settings can use after parental permission and schedule availability have been determined.

Delucia-Waack (2006) developed general selection criteria for psychoeducation groups with children and adolescents. These criteria include (a) similar age range (within 2 years to match development); (b) siblings in different groups; (c) heterogeneity of problem issues; (d) select and link members based on group topic; (e) no history of conflict among potential members, to ensure compatibility in psychoeducational format; and (f) balance so that each member has someone with whom to connect and someone to serve as a role model. Delucia-Waack also developed a screening criteria grid including group goals, selection and deselection criteria based on group goals, questions related to screening criteria, and information regarding member fit to the group. Delucia-Waack suggested the following sequence for screening interviews.

- Introduce group leaders, purpose of the screening interview, procedural details and group goals
- Potential members' group goals
- Group procedures and ground rules regarding attendance, out-of-group contacts, confidentiality, for example

- Commitment to ground rules
- Information on how groups work, leader and member roles, and specific activities
- Identification of how each member can work on his or her goals
- Specific selection or deselection criteria
- How each member can contribute to the group
- Concerns about group participation
- Final selection process (pp. 59–61)

Information About the Leader

Leader information about scope of practice, the general goals of the group, group techniques used, style of interaction, use of one or more coleaders, and successful member behaviors desired can assist potential members in screening themselves into or out of the group pool and in providing the group leader with information on match of group goals to member needs.

Research-Based Screening Instruments

Group Selection Questionnaire

Krogel, Beecher, Presnell, Burlingame, and Simonsen (2009) conducted a qualitative study on very high (those who might do poorly in group) and very low (those who might do well) scorers on the Group Selection Questionnaire (GSQ) to help determine differences between the two groups. A further purpose was to understand how the instrument can be used to identify those who might do well in group and, for those likely to do poorly, how to make the group more effective. The authors compared clinical (users of the counseling and career center) and nonclinical (students in a general education psychology course) responders in the high- and low-scoring groups and supplemented the data with content analysis of follow-up interviews. Analyses

> indicated that low scorers anticipated benefits from groups, found it easy to share feelings and opinions, felt they were a part of groups, and described themselves as open. High scorers reported being passive, private, reserved, and unlikely to share feelings. (p. 529)

Krogel et al. found response differences between the clinical and nonclinical responders in that low-scoring nonclinical participants reported greater activity and less inhibition than did the clinical group.

In her research on the GSQ 3.0, Baker (2010) conducted a validation study of the 19-item screening instrument with college counseling center clients at a conservative university. Baker's study confirmed the validity of the instrument and found it to be generally consistent in its usefulness with the longer 45-item Group Therapy Questionnaire (MacNair-Semands, 2002, 2007). Baker recommended that the GSQ subscales of expectancy for positive outcome and participation hold most promise for pregroup preparation for potential group therapy clients. The third subscale relating to domineering demeanor did not correlate with the Group Therapy Questionnaire.

Learning Style Inventory

In working with task groups in a university project-based course, Kyprianidou, Demetriadis, Tsiatsos, and Pombortsis (2012) developed a group screening and heterogeneous selection model based on learning styles. Kyprianidou and colleagues used a web-based system to aid senior college students (27 male, 23 female) in identifying their individual learning styles, employing a problem-solving styles inventory. The researchers then assigned students to teacher-facilitated, heterogeneous groups distributed across the learning styles. Task group members used their own and others' learning styles to inform their work throughout their project development. The heterogeneous assignment of students to task groups contributed to enhanced collaboration and increased student awareness of how learning styles affected group dynamics. In evaluating student responses to the learning style–based group formation, Kyprianidou and colleagues found, in considering the relative merits of diversity on productivity, "that diversity is more beneficial when the type of the teamwork requires creativity and innovation rather than routine tasks" (p. 105).

Learning Exercise

Sample Interview

You and a colleague are developing a group for the local hospital that will provide support and information to patients who have been diagnosed with cancer and have a reasonably good chance of survival. Construct an interview that could realistically portray a potential group member talking to the group leaders. Provide sufficient details that demonstrate the leader's attention to full disclosure to the patient. Also, ensure the patient's fit with the group purpose and goals. Within the counseling dialogue, you may add the details of the group to ensure that your reader sees clearly how well you as the leaders are providing information and obtaining different types of information about the patient. The dialogue should contain at least two pages (double-spaced) and no more than four pages of comments back and forth.

5

Select

Communication is of utmost importance in meaningful group function-ing. Successful group members are often cited as those who contribute to group processes, are motivated to receive benefit from the group, maintain a willingness to make attendance and participation a priority, and interact reasonably well with others (Anderson, John, Kelter, & Kring, 2001). The description of what is considered a group deviant, on the other hand, entailed an inability to benefit from the group experience, an inability or unwillingness to accept personal responsibility, and a lack of personal aware-ness in an interactional setting. Yalom (2005) represented numerous exclu-sion criteria for member selection, considering that research has provided few inclusion criteria other than the topical aspect of the proposed group.

Selection is not a one-sided process. Gladding (2008) noted that along with the group leader conducting a prescreening process for inclusion, the group member is also given an opportunity through the process to deter-mine if the group is suitable and of interest to him or her personally. As a group leader, you may be asked how you will decide who fits into your group. Through the screening process, potential members are assessed for readiness, motivation to change, willingness to participate with effort, and clinical reasons why the group would not be considered the best modality for therapeutic change (American Group Psychotherapy Association, 2007b; Corey, Corey, & Corey, 2010). It may be obvious at this point that the group leader must have some insight and judgment on which to rely in selecting people who will make up an effective group. Leader training must include mentoring and supervision to support this important element of the member selection process.

Gans and Counselman (2010) identified a variable that may influence both the screening and the selection processes, which is the therapist's countertransference. The authors cited research that confirms what we know about how much the group outcome is impacted by a multitude of factors before the group ever begins. Noted, particularly, was the commonly viewed pressure of therapists to maintain group census or of insurance involvement in the form of financial pressure on client and/or therapist.

Another consideration about referral networks ties in with countertransference when the therapist is concerned about the referral source and ultimate decision to include or exclude. At times, decisions are made to select a group member when external pressures overtake the therapist's better judgment.

In their 1997 research study on how leaders choose counseling group members, Riva, Lippert, and Tackett (2000) looked not only at methods used (previously discussed in Chapter 4) but also at the key variables group leaders employed. They found that match with the group theme was the variable most frequently used (85.3%) to select members. A distant second was the person's compatibility with other members selected (64%), followed by client motivation for personal change (56%), individual's enthusiasm about attending and expectations that the group would help (each at 50.7%), and other variables. They stated, "It appears that leaders endorse selecting group members because of certain interpersonal characteristics" (p. 162). When asked to identify how they measured the variables, Riva and colleagues found this: "Almost exclusively, group leaders used intuition, observation, and client report to determine whether the client possessed the specific characteristic." (p. 163). Only 3% of the professionals surveyed used an objective measure to assist them.

In an updated review, Riva, Wachtel, and Lasky (2004) suggested, "Until more specific selection criteria are identified and formal selection instruments are developed, group leaders may want to ask questions during the selection process that address potential members' relationships with others" (p. 39). In the years since the Riva et al. (2000) survey, there have been significant advances in the construction and validation of research-based selection instruments and outcome measures focusing on intrapersonal and interpersonal variables.

Selection Instruments

Current research on groups is aided by continuing development and refinement of a number of instruments to increase the effectiveness of group selection, to more accurately measure beneficial member outcomes, and to deepen understanding of group processes (Barlow, Burlingame, & Fuhriman, 2005; Burlingame, Kapetanovic, & Ross, 2005). Burlingame, Cox, Davies, Layne, and Gleave (2011) studied the Group Selection Questionnaire (GSQ) as a tool for group leaders to select and compose groups. Much in line with the previously noted criteria for inclusion, group members respond to three subscales of expectancy, participation, and demeanor. The expectancy subscale enables leaders to understand to what degree the potential group member believes in the benefit of the group experience. Attitudes and skills about interpersonal interactions are assessed through the participation subscale. Additionally, the demeanor subscale enables the group leader to ascertain some degree of group deviance, or possible threatening behaviors that would lead to negative group processes, such as talking over others, inappropriate disclosure, or monopolizing conversation. Through self-reported client characteristics, potential group members revealed predictable behaviors such as premature dropout (Burlingame et al., 2011).

Chapman (2010) conducted a study to measure group therapist effectiveness in (a) predicting member outcome, (b) determining the quality of the therapeutic relationship, and (c) their own use of empirically supported group interventions. In his study, Chapman found that group therapists are poor predictors of each of these variables, in similar fashion to previous results with individual therapists. His study of group therapists from a university counseling center and a state hospital also supported the use of measure-based feedback that might assist group leaders in determining who might most benefit from group therapy.

Krogel, Beecher, Presnell, Burlingame, and Simonsen (2009) studied the GSQ as a way to predict who would benefit from group treatment. The assessment of client interpersonal behaviors, goals, and motivation has been shown to have some success in predicting group outcomes with the Group Therapy Questionnaire (MacNair-Semands, 2002), but that tool requires 45 minutes for each participant. To utilize a shorter period for potential group participant and therapist, Davies and Burlingame created the GSQ. As with other research findings (Davies, Seaman, Burlingame, & Layne, 2002; MacNair-Semands, 2002), the participants' expectations for benefit from the group showed as highly significant to a positive outcome, along with their willingness to engage in the group's activities and discussions and to what degree the participants demonstrated domineering behaviors. These three factors were highlighted in studies of the GSQ, identified as expectancy, participation, and domineering (Krogel et al., 2009).

MacNair-Semands (2002) offered evidence that cognitive and behavioral factors relate to both a member's group attendance and participation. The interpersonal factor of social phobia/inhibition evidenced to predict poor attendance, indicating that engaging the group or certain group members may be significantly anxiety producing. Difficulties with social relationships create challenges in group settings seen as behaviors that are less engaged, nonparticipative, and may show in somatic complaints, for example (MacNair-Semands, 2002). Members who scored significantly as angry/hostile were also identified as members who might choose to vent hostility by not attending the group meetings. Expressions of anger or threatening behaviors may be seen and are problematic for process management by the group leader as well as for other group members. These emotions are demonstrated through behavioral responses to what is happening within the group.

A variety of other assessments could be utilized to assess variables identified for success in a given group. In selecting group members, the leader could consider implications that personality traits have on people's interpersonal relationships. For example, the Self-Compassion Scale (Neff, 2003, as cited in Baker & McNulty, 2011) would measure individuals' abilities to experience ranges of self-kindness to self-judgment, thoughts of common humanity to feelings of isolation, and mindful acceptance to overidentification with faults (Baker & McNulty, 2011). Conflicting research has reported that self-compassion either enhances personal relationships or may actually lead to relationship problems. The concern resides in the possible decrease in motivation for correcting interpersonal mistakes.

Baker and McNulty (2011) studied romantic relationships with interaction between self-compassion and conscientiousness. Their results found that these interactions predicted relationship outcomes. Conscientiousness is a subscale in the Big Five Personality Inventory–Short (Goldberg, 1999) and was understood as intrapersonal motivation and analyzed as a moderating factor in relationship satisfaction. This inventory and at least this one subscale could be used to identify individuals' thinking about their relationship interactions and levels of satisfaction while also considering their willingness to be held accountable for their outcomes.

Another type of assessment was found in Kampmeier and Simon's (2001) study measuring independence and differentiation as group processes in group formation and individualization. The authors created a questionnaire and tested it more than once to verify their theory of individuality as two distinct components of not only self-perception but also the perception of others. Kampmeier and Simon contended that rather than two antagonistic concepts, group formation and individualization are relational, and group formation is "facilitated to the extent that is compatible with the expression of individuality" (p. 452). The study also analyzed group formation in light of multicultural contexts, focused on majority–minority intergroup interactions.

Gosling, Rentfrow, and Swann (2003) reported on brief versions of the Big-Five personality domains, which could be useful in obtaining ratings of self-esteem that could translate into interpersonal behaviors. Extreme responses on any of the bipolar scales could assist group leaders in selecting potential group members. Gosling et al. grouped items from multiple assessments into five categories:

- Extraverted, enthusiastic (sociable, assertive, talkative, active, NOT reserved, or shy)
- Agreeable, kind (trusting, generous, sympathetic, cooperative, NOT aggressive, or cold)
- Dependable, organized (hard working, responsible, self-disciplined, thorough, NOT careless, or impulsive)
- Emotionally stable, calm (relaxed, self-confident, NOT anxious, moody, easily upset, or easily stressed)
- Open to experience, imaginative (curious, reflective, creative, deep, open-minded, NOT conventional) (p. 508)

Personality variables are often related to academic and job performance and job satisfaction (Betz & Borgen, 2010). In line with concepts of positive psychology and healthy personality, Betz and Borgen's study analyzed

personality traits to find that three dimensions affect performance and satisfaction outcomes. Conscientiousness measured productivity styles, extraver-
sion measured interpersonal styles, and neuroticism measured intrapersonal
styles. In selecting group members, the dimensions noted may predict beneficial group behaviors and attitudes.

Paper-and-pencil assessments alone are not always sufficient in determining potential group members. For example, consider this recent e-mail about
exclusion from treatment based on a personal style instrument:

*I was asked the question: (1) Can the Myers-Briggs be used to determine
whether a person is an introvert, and (2) if the person is basically an introvert, can the Myers-Briggs be used as a basis for explaining a client not
participating within a substance abuse treatment group?*

*Clients are being discontinued from the substance abuse program for not
participating in group. The apparent expectation seems to be that they will
come into group and open up. If they do not contribute verbally, then they
are viewed as not participating. Resultantly, they are discharged as "not
participating." Research bears that the natural process for groups tends to be
for deviants (i.e., quiet/introverted) to be put out, if they do not voluntarily
exit, as they are seen as slowing the group process as they are not function-
ally similar.*

*Multiple factors can influence a client showing up for group as well as not
verbally participating in the process. While clinicians use tools to determine
whether a client is a "good fit" for a group, success within the group is
uncertain. From the research that I have done (less than extensive), standard
psychological tests have failed to yield valid predictions for group behavior.
Thus, a test cannot predict client success within a treatment group.*

*What would be your arguments—pros-cons—on using the Myers-Briggs
explaining a client not participating in a treatment group? Do you have
other points that I can use during a consult on this subject?*

Self-report assessments offer the participant's perception, but interviews
add a professional clinical or academic perspective to the assessment process.
A finding that came out of Krogel et al.'s (2009) qualitative study showed
that people who scored low on the GSQ would be considered as potential
participants, but those who scored high would be possibly screened out.
However, the interesting note was that those who might be screened out
based solely on the assessment may be those who clinically would benefit a
great deal from the interpersonal and social activities of the group. In the
above e-mail example, this conflict is demonstrated. Because the group member in question did not verbally participate in the group and was perceived
as an introvert, participation in the treatment program was terminated. This
participant may be motivated to participate in other ways not measured by
the paper-and-pencil instrument. Depending on the group leader's needs for
immediacy and to maximize referrals and group matching, pregroup preparation is encouraged for those potential members who do not score as positive predictors. This result shows the sensitive nature of the processes of
screening and preparation.

Research has shown that leader and member dynamics are the strongest indicators of predictable outcomes (Forsyth, 2010; Krogel et al., 2009; MacNair-Semands, 2002; Yalom, 2005). Yalom (2005) summarized that the group's attraction to members correlates with positive therapeutic outcomes. Key to the group's effectiveness is the perception of group cohesiveness. Burlingame, Fuhriman, and Johnson (2001) explained that cohesiveness involves the aggregated relationships within a group, consisting of leader and member relationships. The group leader must prepare for the interpersonal processes that create the best possible group environment. Attention to pregroup preparation increases member satisfaction by presenting a better conceptualization of group member roles so that members feel empowered. Expectations are set forth, and members learn what is needed for group cohesion.

Learning Exercise

Selection Instruments

Develop a selection instrument rationale for the following potential group members. You may create an instrument, use one that has been described in this chapter, or apply another you found in your research. In any case, you must provide a rationale that describes your decision-making process about how the instrument will benefit the selection process for your group.

The group you are forming is a personal growth group for adult females. The group's purpose is to provide a safe learning environment for these women to develop self-reflection skills and basic skills in three mindfulness practices.

Jenna—Extraverted, sociable, and talkative, with a warm disposition and apparently trusting nature. She describes herself as dependable and hardworking, generally calm. She states that she is open to the group idea because she wants to learn more about herself, with the goal of enhancing her creativity. Described as a bit of a nerd, Jenna wants to become more in tune with herself and others, and believes that the mindfulness practices will benefit her in remaining calm at work, which is becoming increasingly stressful.

Harriet—A bit shy, warm disposition, and tentative with the group leader's questions. She describes herself as compassionate and desires to help others in the world but frequently avoids large groups of people because she does not believe she fits in well. She is conscientious and hardworking but is rather quiet unless addressed first. Once questioned, however, Harriet has a great deal to say about philanthropic activities and social justice issues in the world. Harriet believes that she would benefit from a group experience to work on her interpersonal interactions and skills in collaboration with others. She desires insight into her occasional loneliness, which she describes as self-imposed. Hesitant to join in many social functions, Harriet finds herself at home with her dog and cat.

6

Compose

Group composition includes a variety of member and leader characteristics that will affect the group's effectiveness and member satisfaction. The group leader selected members based on myriad criteria and now must compose the group to achieve the desired goal.

For example, depending on whether the group is all male or all female or mixed gender, the level of disclosure will be impacted. This interactive effect will have intended and unintended effects on the group outcome and level of satisfaction of the group members. At times, such as in cases of mandated participation, individual choice, or other factors, we are not always able to choose the group members.

Open vs. Closed Groups

A major consideration that will influence how comfortably group members interact is whether the group has open versus closed membership. It is possible that the group will be energized with new members, but other groups may express feelings of violation from the presence of occasional new members. Even if there is a sense of violation, a skilled group leader can use the response as a productive tool in helping the group redesign its process.

Homogeneity or heterogeneity is one decision that greatly impacts the group composition. Besides selecting members who relate to the purpose of the group in a significant way, leaders may choose members who share other characteristics, such as gender. To some degree, members will have some personal characteristics in common but will also experience differences, for example, in coping strategies. Some amount of diversity ensures that members have opportunities to learn from one another's perspectives and experiences.

Wilkinson and Fung (2002) noted that homogeneous groups in education affected students' learning outcomes, due to peer effects from a normative environment where members contributed to the group processes in dynamic leader–member interaction. They also pointed out that heterogeneous groups offer variations in multiple student factors, such as ability, gender, or diversity, so that peer effects generate discourse from the intragroup interactions that lead to "cognitive restructuring, cognitive rehearsal, problem solving, and other forms of higher-level thinking" (p. 425). Students' perceptions of their influence within the group also created differences in their group interactions, impacting the overall group dynamic.

Conyne (1999) and Conyne, Crowell, and Newmeyer (2008), among many others, have emphasized best practices in planning to appropriately prepare group members—specifically, obtaining informed consent and outlining the limits of confidentiality. Yalom (2005) presented several points to include a brief explanation of the meaning of therapy in general and how all people who seek help are attempting to gratify some relationship in their lives. Yalom goes on to describe to members that groups are "social laboratories" (p. 300) where interactions have potential application to the relationships outside the group as well. One way to instill hope and faith in the group process is to emphasize the benefits of group therapy with assurances of respect and positive regard as a basis for the ground rules (Capuzzi, Gross, & Stauffer, 2010; Gladding, 2008; Johnson & Johnson, 2003; Tang & Bashir, 2012; Yalom, 2005). Ground rules work well when collaboration with the group members solidifies a form of commitment to the overall purpose and tasks of the group. Ecologically, the concept of collaboration continues past the first group meeting; rules can, therefore, be added, deleted, or modified.

Setting limits is another aspect of orienting the group members to acceptable boundaries of behavior to promote a positive environment. Gladding (2008) stated that limits can be set not only within the ground rules but with leader behaviors and leadership style that establish firm, fair, and friendly interactions. Wubbolding (2000) considers the environment as a firm but friendly atmosphere for establishing the counseling relationship not only by setting boundaries but also through discussion of consequences when using reality therapy as a theoretical orientation. Similarly, the type of relationship that is preferred can come only from the group members individually. Their motivation to have a positive growth experience is greatly enhanced when they make the inner choice to change.

Orientation to the group is recommended by numerous experts (Conyne et al., 2008; Corey, Corey, & Corey, 2010; Delucia-Waack, 2006; Gladding, 2008; Yalom, 2005). Many decisions were made in the planning phase and will ultimately drive the group's composition. Decisions included the population to be served; homogeneous or heterogeneous membership; the setting conducive to working with the particular population; access for all involved; time, size, and frequency of meetings; length of the group; whether it is open or closed; and more details about curriculum and materials and resources needed. Prior to the work of the group, however, orienting the group members to these details and others increases the chances that the group will run effectively.

Informed consent is one aspect of orienting the group members. Typically, a broad overview with all basic information about group work in general is included, which assists individuals in their decision to join the group and to what degree they will participate (Corey et al., 2010). At the same time, a professional disclosure statement may be provided, which in counseling presents the leader's credentials, training and qualifications, and contact information. Information about fees, insurance, members' rights and responsibilities, and details regarding absences or standardized rules might be included as well, and often there is a brief description of the leader's theoretical orientation and professional affiliations. Most important, information on the limits of confidentiality is offered to ensure that the group member is able to review what is explained in person, either in a pregroup meeting or the first group meeting.

A pregroup meeting is commonly used to orient group members. The structure of that meeting is likely to be somewhat different, however, in that the group leader is much more directive than in subsequent meetings, when more member input is desired. Just as Lewin (as cited in Wittenbaum et al., 2004) suggested, a group relates to its environment with varying levels of adaptation, and to the degree to which the group's boundaries are permeable, interactions within the group can be flexible and directed. Group leaders, therefore, can establish from the outset the type of environment that allows for individuality and adaptability without members feeling oppressed or not valued. With the leaders' invitation for input, group members can receive information when appropriate but also provide their own wishes for group rules, for example.

Learning Exercise

Test Your Organizational Skills: Ecological Checklist

The purpose of this exercise is to practice organizational skills that will enhance the effectiveness of the group you are forming. Complete the chart below, placing the items in the list in appropriate boxes. Feel free to add details as you see fit.

In my group formation, I have considered the following:

- Gender
- Language barriers
- Race
- National origin
- Socioeconomic status
- Education level
- Social network
- Influences of managed care

Ecological Components	Place Items From List Below	Notes (Place page numbers or citations from the chapters or other documents of import)
Context: External and group factors that influence the group and members		
Meaning making: Ways members make meaning of experiences and environment		
Interconnections: Quality of member-to-member and member-to-leader interactions		
Collaboration: Work that helps the group move forward		
Social system maintenance: Creating and supporting a group culture		

- Group time limits
- Cultural influences
- Values and morals (and the effects of these on behavior)
- Disability—physical, mental, or emotional handicap
- Age of members
- Makeup and level of support or influence of group members
- Makeup and level of support or influence of family members
- Image of self in context with the world
- Management support
- Manpower
- Materials
- Methods
- Funding (money)
- Roles clients have within society: family, workplace, school, church, and community
- Expectations and behaviors associated with positions members hold in society
- Environmental systems (e.g., school, community)
- Group goals
- Group type (task, psychoeducational, counseling, or therapy)

- Group purpose (prevention, development, remediation, problem solving)
- Organization rules and regulations
- Recognition of change for self and others
- State or provincial laws and practice regulations
- Limits of confidentiality in group work
- Supervisor qualifications in group work
- Member expectations of change
- Recruiting, screening, and selecting participants
- Leader training and level of expertise
- Range and variety of group activities to be implemented
- Application of group learning to life

7

Case Examples

In this chapter, we provide you with two case examples of the formation process in action. You will note in each example that we have included case background, ecological consideration of factors, and detailed information at each of the substeps—organizing, marketing and recruiting, screening, selecting, and composing. These examples can serve as models for your own group formation efforts. You will notice that each case requires differential attention at each planning stage, including varied resources, different organization structures, and contrasting strategies for group construction in real-world settings.

Forming Study Groups

In this example, an educator in the counseling program at a state university has considered small groups to be an effective strategy for students to learn both the leadership and membership aspects of group participation. Fuhriman and Burlingame (2001) studied training for group work to discover that there has been a discrepancy between the desire for and provision of group treatment in clinical practice and the inconsistent curriculum of training group leaders. A significant finding in their research showed that expected demand for groups did not increase the levels of training in group leadership. The educator is intentional here to convey value in the practice and leadership responsibilities of group work.

Perusse, Goodnough, and Lee (2009) offered four main ways that professionals can weave group work into their current practices, specifically in an educational setting. To begin with, there needs to be consultation for a broad systems approach of support for the group model. Ecologically, the context of the proposed group is an educational setting. The group focus is to be the creation of study sessions for topical discussions within an ethics course. The common objective to include ethical discussion papers on topics, along with a shared commitment to produce the group paper, demonstrates what

Conyne, Rapin, and Rand (2008) identified as team work. Within the course curriculum, the group component adds the ecological factors of interdependence and collaboration to the students' learning experiences as they utilize a team approach to their assignments.

Another key way for the educator to practice with groups is to commit to preparation that considers the impact of time, energy, and resources to the full extent of the group planning process (Capuzzi, Gross, & Stauffer, 2010; Perusse et al., 2009; Thomas & Pender, 2008, Sec. A.3.b). Just as educators prepare for academic curricula, group leadership requires similar goals, objectives (Thomas & Pender, 2008, Sec. A.4.b), and allotment of resources for effective group work that supports the educational program with rigor and professionalism. Other ecological concerns in the group preparation process included physical space and materials, access to restroom facilities, parking, timing of the sessions around classes in the building, and other details, also included in the checklist in this chapter (Singh, Merchant, Skudrzyk, & Ingene, 2012, Sec. I.b; Thomas & Pender, 2008, A.5). Jacobs, Masson, and Harvill (2009) repeatedly emphasized the importance of planning efforts for group leaders to consider and ultimately prioritize choices about the proposed experience for leaders and members.

An interesting aspect of the ecological assessment for incorporating group work into an educational environment, and another way for this educator to weave group work into practice, includes exploration of institutional policies (Perusse et al., 2009). Ongoing collaboration with policymakers and administrators enhances the continuation of opportunities to utilize group work in an institution so that there is no perception of abuse within that institutional system. From the initial conceptualization of a group strategy, the educator in this example identified support from many of the college's faculty but discovered that one administrator did not value the group concept as tied to the learner-centered strategic planning that had been recently implemented within the college. A professional imperative for this educator, therefore, became an advocacy project to inform the system's administration of the potential for enhanced learning by students who engage in teamwork and collaboration through professionally led group experiences (Whiston & Quinby, 2009). In the meantime, the educator incorporated throughout the quarter assignments requiring group study sessions for preparing group responses to ethical topics of discussion.

Training in group leadership also was identified as an important counseling skill that would benefit the university students in their overall program, particularly the school counseling students. Perusse et al. (2009) emphasized this importance when they concluded their four suggestions for weaving group work into a school counseling program.

With significant time constraints in school settings, school counselors require artful solutions to student problems, often utilizing group work to accomplish goals with more students in short time frames (Crowell, Sebera, & Coaston, 2012). Secondary, middle, or elementary school groups require parental permission for participation, as well as coordination with other elements of the school system processes, such as administrative and teacher acceptance, release of students from classes, and space use.

The educator used her research to construct group work so that the students received an ethical dilemma, but within each group they could determine the format and resources for their discussion with the rest of the class. To some degree, the students fleshed out the ethical dilemma with details from their own experiences or readings and then chose from a variety of models to present an ethical decision-making process and possible solution. In this way, the educator believed that group empowerment would facilitate the necessary collaboration for the creation and presentation of their ethical dilemma. To add interest to the group functioning, the educator required groups to establish a reporter, who would present the group's work. The term *leader* was not used, but in her experience she had found that the reporter often took a leadership role to prepare. Another facet of the group's decision was tying the group grade to the individual's engagement in the task assigned. Periodic assessment was used randomly, whereby the educator sat with the working group to determine the group climate and levels of participation. Following best practice guidelines included previous classroom time spent discussing the various group roles, leadership skills, group environment and developmental stages, and interpersonal relationships so that all students received the training prior to performing their assignments.

Meaningfulness is functionality (Bonito & Sanders, 2010), which means that the instructor's presentation of the assignment impacts the ability of students not only to weigh the costs and benefits of particular solutions but also to collaborate with one another on managing, prioritizing, focusing, and interrelating the problem they have before them. As an aspect of group formation, the instructor needs to emphasize the meaning of the assignment to the overall practice of counseling and the training to be effective. An outgrowth of the assignment could be to further discussion on course group work in comparison to group work in a community agency.

Organize

Ecological Background

The context of the proposed group is an educational setting within a large university in a counselor training program. The group focus is to be the creation of study sessions for topical discussions within an ethics course. The common objective is to comprise ethical discussion papers on topics, along with a shared commitment to produce a group paper. From the initial conceptualization of a group strategy, the educator in this example identified support from many of the college's faculty, but one administrator did not value the group concept. The educator believes that the group work is an excellent match with both the accreditation standards for counselor training and best practices of training group leaders.

Resources

Time

A key to preparation considers the impact of time and energy. The educator is dedicated to the counseling training program full-time in her role as university faculty. She teaches three courses, including the ethics course and the group work course. Timing of the sessions around classes in the building may have impacted noise level, which is a consideration.

Management Support

The educator has the ability to determine her teaching practices within reason. She has considered class structure as an element in her course planning that also aligns with professional and educational competencies. The creation of the groups does not entail any additional support except to indicate that the type of learning varies from traditionally led courses in the college. The fact that one administrator did not value the group concept was a concern, but research provides a strong indication of positive academic outcomes that can be used as references.

Manpower

No additional manpower is needed for the educator to run her group-structured course. She will consider the use of her own time divided among the various student groups, with occasional feedback and checking in on the ethics problem and on the functioning of the groups specifically.

Materials

Other ecological concerns in the group preparation process included physical space and materials, access to restroom facilities, parking, and other details. The university provides the classroom with movable seating and access to restrooms that can accommodate disabled persons, but parking at the university is an ongoing problem. Some students must park several blocks away and walk, which must be considered in their timeliness to classes and meetings. The instructor provides a number of simple evaluation instruments that are brief but provide some information for the groups as they assess their own work together. The ethics problems are incorporated within the course readings.

Methods

The groups are task groups, as they are problem-solving ethics cases. The groups may utilize professional literature or popular media, such as magazine or newspaper articles, to demonstrate key points in their ethics cases. Members individually provide input to the group's case, but one member is selected to report to the other groups and to the instructor about the group's conclusions. As a counselor educator and group specialist, the educator uses a best practice approach and periodically infuses established guidelines to create awareness of the group processes.

Money

No additional money is needed in the performance of the course groups. Students already have textbooks from which to obtain their cases and access to the university library for additional reference materials.

Market and Recruit

There is no need to market for and recruit group participants, as the ethics course is a mandatory course for all counseling students.

Screen

The educator does not utilize a formal screening process, because the group of students in the course is determined by their mandatory requirement to obtain the graduate credits for studying group counseling. However, not all student groups run well, so one decision made by the educator is to withhold group selection for 2 weeks to observe students' interactions within the course room. The educator has the option to allow students to self-select their groups, randomize the groups each week, or establish fixed groups over the entire 16-week semester. Since research has shown the importance of member commitment to the group, the educator decided to keep fixed groups over the entire semester. She also wanted to randomize the group members, allowing for a caveat that an obvious potentially problematic personality match may be overruled before divulging the group member lists.

Select

Though we stated that selection is not a one-sided process, in an educational setting, the educator often makes decisions for the best interest of all students, rather than the personal needs of any one student. However, if a student determines that a group is unsuitable for some reason, the student is able to discuss the issue with the educator privately. The educator has decided to allow the groups to make two decisions of their own: (a) Each group decides whether the reporter will always be the same person, and (b) each group selects its own reporter.

Compose

Training in group work is included in the first 2 weeks of the semester so that all students are considered potential group leaders, as well as group members. The important question will be, "How will you decide how well you as the leader fit into your group?" This pregroup preparation assists the students in understanding how to consider members for readiness, motivation to change, willingness to participate with effort, and clinical reasons why the group would not be considered the best modality for therapeutic change in a clinical setting.

Case Example: Working With Street Women

Bonnie is a licensed social worker employed by a large human service agency in a metropolitan area. With 30 years of experience working with drug and alcohol programs, Bonnie has performed numerous professional roles in her career. Among them are serving as a prevention specialist with at-risk youth, conducting psychoeducation groups on prevention and education about drugs and alcohol, serving as a therapist in a residential treatment facility for women, doing intake assessments, and making treatment referrals to a number of agencies, among other responsibilities. Bonnie is in her 15th year at her current social service agency and is feeling some conflict about her future work and education goals. She has been planning to go back for her master's degree but has delayed her plans because of family health concerns that have taken most of her spare time. Bonnie has been reflecting on her professional path and wants to contribute to the community in a way that continues to celebrate her own recovery path of 20 drug-free years, and to serve an underrepresented population.

Reflecting on her work experience, Bonnie identified group work as most rewarding and talked about her current group work with special alcohol- and drug-abuse populations. She facilitates three kinds of group every week: a support group at her agency facility for participants in alcohol recovery, an evening transitional support psychoeducation group for drop-in participants on the treatment waiting list, and a weekly open psychoeducation group at a women's shelter.

Her 1 day per week with this third population of homeless women surviving prostitution, mental illness, and drug addiction is what most inspires

Bonnie. She plans to complete her master's degree and specialize in group work with women on the streets. The women Bonnie serves remind her of herself at an earlier time in her life. She, too, became addicted and lost her marriage, children, home, job, and self-respect. She was able to regain all she had lost through drug treatment centers and 12-step programs. She received encouragement, love, and respect from providers and fellow support group members until she was able to love herself again. Bonnie's social work training inspired her to work in alcohol- and drug-abuse settings. In her current work with women at the shelter, Bonnie observed that the women had been ill for such a long time, and in a vicious cycle of addiction, prostitution, and life in the criminal justice system, that they were immobile. As in her previous group work in alcohol- and drug-dependence treatments, Bonnie emphasizes that the women may die from the disease of addiction but that they do not have to. Her commitment to the women at the shelter is to educate, not to judge. Bonnie expresses her love for the women she serves. She can see good and beauty in them that others may not see. Let us look at this work assignment through the lens of the formation steps.

Organize

Ecological Background

The agency employing Bonnie as a member of a consortium that addresses broad community physical and mental health needs. The consortium identifies underserved populations and needs, and then matches them with community resources to minimize service duplication. Within this orientation, Bonnie feels an excellent match with her social work training that emphasized community-based treatments and social justice principles.

Resources

Time

In her 8 hours per week dedicated to the group program, Bonnie has sufficient time to plan and conduct her group. However, she is occasionally pulled from that assignment to fill in at her home agency when needed to facilitate an ongoing group. The women's shelter provides safe harbor and all living supports while the participants gain skills to transfer from street survival to permanent housing, employment, or education, and family reconciliation. The average stay per resident is 1 year.

Management Support

While Bonnie is not responsible for agency resources, she knows that a great deal of coordination contributed to the formation of the program for homeless prostitutes. The creation of the program stemmed from jail over-crowding and recognition of the cyclical pattern in the population: drug use, prostitution, arrest, jail time, release, and repeat. Thirty people from 20 social service agencies, alcohol- and drug-treatment agencies, funders, the criminal justice system, and community members worked as a planning group to establish broad understanding of the scope and depth of the con-cerns of the identified women and proposed funding for a dedicated pro-gram. Initial funding provided housing and treatment for a group of about 30 women. Community fundraising and additional grants have provided continued fiscal support.

Manpower

The treatment program for homeless prostitutes is one among several services provided at a residential shelter for single women. A program direc-tor, managers, and staff are assigned to the free-standing program. An intake and outreach coordinator interfaces with the criminal justice system to iden-tify eligible women. Bonnie's agency has assigned her to the residential shel-ter 1 day per week as part of the consortium resources. Bonnie conducts groups and helps coordinate additional service referrals for the women in her group. In addition to paid staff and resources provided by agencies such as Bonnie's employer, the residential shelter has a number of peer volunteers to serve as mentors. These volunteers are graduates of the program and serve as successful models of recovery from heroin and other substance addiction and prostitution. Program participants are encouraged to continue participa-tion in regular meetings both at the women's shelter and with other agencies and support groups after their graduation from the program.

Materials

The residential shelter provides meeting space as part of the homelike atmosphere of the shelter. For her group, Bonnie provides a number of mate-rials to assist the women in moving from lives of trauma and instability to lives worth saving, including inspirational movies and recordings to stimu-late positive conversation. Examples include films on addiction and recovery (e.g., *Losing Isaiah, 28 Days*, and *When a Man Loves a Woman*), TV series (e.g., *Brinks Place*), CDs, and printed materials. Bonnie's group plan incor-porates themes and planned group activities to organize sessions.

Methods

The group is psychoeducational and support focused. The open group sessions are topic centered and include addiction, sobriety, acquisition of permanent housing, reunification with children and families, employment, education, and daily-living coping strategies. For example, group members use magazine articles and pictures to demonstrate their past, present, and desired future. Members individually share their stories and hang their completed collages in their rooms. Bonnie is impressed with the extent to which members share their goals and dreams. In some of the sessions, members can simply enjoy the time to interact with other women who share similar struggles.

The participating agencies use a best practice approach and include detailed screening, referral, record keeping, and research on program success using established guidelines. Bonnie uses agency-supplied tools for recording group and individual progress.

Machines

The shelter provides playback equipment for films and CDs.

Money

Bonnie's employer pays her salary for the assignment at the women's shelter. Housing and daily-living supports for program participants are provided by the shelter. Additional mental health, alcohol and drug treatment, education, and employment resources are provided by other agencies in coordination with the shelter. Grants and donations continue to fund the services.

Market and Recruit

Several strategies are employed to publicize the program. When prostitutes engage the justice system, whether at the time of arrest or upon release, they are provided with information about the program. Community agencies, public health clinics, hospitals, mental health centers, and physicians provide information to potential candidates. Women are also able to nominate themselves for participation in the program.

Recruiting is accomplished through the referral sources above and through direct contact with the target population. The outreach/intake coordinator routinely visits prostitutes on the street to see how they are doing and to offer the support and services of the shelter. Women are invited to participate in a group just to feel better if they are not ready to commit to the full residential program. Women are encouraged to call the intake coordinator just to touch base on how they are doing. The inability to see themselves free from drug addiction and the related prostitution is a common barrier to admission to the program. Potential participants are encouraged to consider the protected environment as a possible escape from their entrapped lives on the street. Police who patrol the densest areas for prostitution know the women from repeated criminal justice contact and encourage program participation in lieu of or following incarceration.

Screen

Heavy documentation is required during the assessment of potential participants using treatment improvement protocols (Substance Abuse and Mental Health Services Administration, 2012). Women have to be single, homeless, addicted, and generally supporting themselves through prostitution to qualify for participation in the program. Unfortunately, many women in the community and in surrounding counties qualify. In general, the women have few marketable skills because of limitations in education, or they are so far removed from employment and relationships that they cannot view themselves as worthy. Many live in abandoned buildings. Any of the many referring sources serve as initial screeners, and then formal screening is accomplished by intake staff.

Select

The most important and challenging selection criterion is the desire to change. As active addicts, potential participants often describe themselves as terrible people. The street women need affirmation from the numerous referring sources that they are worthy people so that they can view a positive future of recovery. When selected, participants can see the possibility of getting their lives back on a healthy path.

Compose

The group is made up of potential program participants who are testing the safety of the treatment program and those who are actively participating in their recovery through formal program participation and housing at the women's shelter. Members of the group also include former program participants who serve as recovery models. A program goal is that the participants be free of drugs and alcohol. Program managers monitor compliance.

Learning Exercise

Applying the Formulation Steps

Using the following example, apply the formulation steps identified in this book to analyze the group work you see.

Katherine is a licensed counselor working within an urban school in a large metropolitan city. She is both a licensed professional counselor and a certified school counselor, but the funding for her job comes through a large federal grant to support a variety of initiatives in inner-city schools with low annual scores on state testing. Katherine has 12 years of experience working in schools—5 years as a school counselor and 7 years with a community agency that placed mental health services in school settings. Katherine has completed a research study that included a prevention effort with at-risk youth. It was a small study to do a brief measure on the effectiveness of a group intervention in the nearby middle school. She offered a series of eight academic skills training group sessions and had the students self-evaluate their improvement. Katherine included grade report data to see if there was improvement in students' coursework, and there was a slight improvement for 85% of the students involved. This was part of the experience that netted her a position with the federal grant under which she will work for 4 years. Her prior group leadership experience also has included conducting psycho-education groups on prevention and education about drugs and alcohol. Katherine has community agency experience as well, as she has worked as a therapist in a treatment facility for teenage girls, doing intake assessments and making treatment referrals to other agencies.

Obtaining the federal grant position has led Katherine to have mixed feelings about her future career goals with regard to obtaining a doctorate to teach counseling and supervision. She has considered this for the past few years but has delayed her plans because of aging parents' health concerns and finances. Katherine wants to contribute to her personal development but also to the counseling profession in ways that support counseling opportunities for school counselors, and to enhance the training of school counselors to achieve that goal. She has even considered a couple of topics that she believes would be excellent dissertations. She has always chosen to work with at-risk students in challenging urban environments, serving to offer hope and support to young people to make choices that will enhance their opportunities in life.

Katherine has found in the past that group work is particularly helpful with young people. She prefers to facilitate small groups of about six youths to effectively nurture and respond to each child's needs. She also has not always been able to locate a qualified group leader to colead, so small groups ensure that she will manage well as a sole leader. She has a heart for disadvantaged youth and their families who live in poverty. Her knowledge of the environment and numbers of young people who do not even complete high school astonishes and saddens her. Many of those youth are academically strong enough but make choices that seem to maintain their socioeconomic position. She has recently included a support group for parents of children in the school where she works to teach parenting skills and offer support so that they might best support their children. Her preference is to work specifically with the parents of students in her small groups, but she is open to helping any adults who are willing to learn about themselves, the education system, and resources within the community. Katherine's network of colleagues touches many helpful services available in the community and accessible to families in the school where she works.

As a part of the grant planning process, Katherine recommended four small groups of middle school students (two seventh grade and two eighth grade) who are particularly at risk of school failure. The identified students have academic weaknesses as well as truancy issues and poor parental involvement. Katherine has access to much of the student data since she is an established professional in the school building, with her own office near the gymnasium. The groups are intended to run during the school day and will be evaluated for research purposes, requiring parental consent.

Concluding Thoughts

Now that you have had the opportunity to read about group formation, and to apply its concepts to exercises in this book, you are ready to apply them to your group plan. The time you spend in this activity will help reduce practice errors in your group. No planning, however sophisticated, can eliminate all potential issues you will encounter in your groups, but it will surely reduce them. The group field is still in its infancy regarding some key questions—for example, What type of group works best for specific populations? Can groups help those with characteristics likely to exclude them? While some answers have been determined, many more are yet to be fully understood. Evidence-based practice supports the continued development of tools for group member selection and evaluation of group effectiveness. As you read the rest of the books in this series, you will notice that planning continues to be central to effective conduct, processing, and supervision of your group. We support you in your efforts.

References _____

Acuff, C., Bennett, B. E., Bricklin, P. M., Canter, M. B., Knapp, S. J., Moldawsky, S., et al. (1999). Considerations for ethical practice in managed care. *Professional Psychology: Research and Practice, 30,* 563–575.

American College Personnel Association. (2006). *Statement of ethical principles and standards.* Washington, DC: Author. Retrieved from http://www.myacpa.org/au/documents/EthicsStatement.pdf

American Counseling Association. (1999). *Ethical standards for Internet on-line counseling.* Retrieved from http://mooramoora.org.au/bobrich/psych/ethical.html

American Counseling Association. (2005). *ACA code of ethics.* Alexandria, VA: Author. Retrieved from http://www.counseling.org/Resources/aca-code-of-ethics.pdf

American Group Psychotherapy Association. (2007a). *Practice guidelines for group therapy: Creating successful therapy groups.* New York: Author.

American Group Psychotherapy Association. (2007b). *Practice guidelines for group therapy: Selection of clients.* New York: Author.

American Group Psychotherapy Association and National Registry of the Certified Group Psychotherapists. (2002). *AGPA and NRCGP guidelines for ethics.* New York: Author.

American Mental Health Counselors Association. (2010). *Code of ethics of the American Mental Health Counselors Association: 2010 revision.* Alexandria, VA: Author. Retrieved from http://www.amhca.org/assets/news/AMHCA_Code_of_Ethics_2010_w_pagination_cxd_51110.pdf

American Psychological Association. (2002). *Ethical principles of psychologists and code of conduct.* Washington, DC: Author. Retrieved from http://www.apa.org/ethics/code/principles.pdf

American Psychological Association. (2010). *Ethical principles of psychologists and code of conduct: 2010 amendments.* Washington, DC: Author.

American School Counselor Association. (2010). *Ethical standards for school counselors.* Alexandria, VA: Author. Retrieved from http://www.schoolcounselor.org/files/EthicalStandards2010.pdf

Anderson, C., John, O., Kelter, D., & Kring, A. (2001). Who attains social status? Effects of personality and physical attractiveness in social groups, *Journal of Personality and Social Psychology, 81,* 116–132.

Association for the Advancement of Social Work with Groups. (2005). *AASWG standards for social work practice with groups* (2nd ed.). New York: Author. Retrieved from http://www.aaswg.org/files/AASWG_Standards_for_Social_Work_Practice_with_Groups.pdf

Baker, E. (2010). *Selecting members for group therapy: A continued validation study of the Group Selection Questionnaire.* Unpublished doctoral dissertation, Brigham Young University, Provo, UT.

Baker, L. R., & McNulty, J. K. (2011). Self-compassion and relationship maintenance: The moderating roles of conscientiousness and gender. *Journal of Personality and Social Psychology, 100,* 853–873.

Bales, R. F. (1999). *Social interaction systems: Theory and measurement.* New Brunswick, NJ: Transition.

Barlow, S. H. (2012). An application of the competency model to group-specialty practice. *Professional Psychology Research and Practice, 43,* 442–451.

Barlow, S. H., Burlingame, G. M., & Fuhriman, A. J. (2005). The history of group practice: A century of knowledge. In S. Wheelan (Ed.), *The handbook of group research and practice* (pp. 39–64). Thousand Oaks, CA: Sage.

Bemak, F., & Conyne, R. K. (2004). Ecological group work. In R. K. Conyne & E. P. Cook (Eds.), *Ecological counseling: An innovative approach to conceptualizing person-environment interaction* (pp. 195–217). Alexandria, VA: American Counseling Association.

Berg, R. C., Landreth, G. L., & Fall, K. A. (2012). *Group counseling: Concepts and procedures* (5th ed.). New York: Routledge.

Bernard, H., Burlingame, G., Flores, P., Greene, L., Joyce, A., Kobos, J., et al. (2008). Clinical practice guidelines for group psychotherapy. *International Journal of Group Psychotherapy, 58,* 455–542.

Betz, N. E., & Borgen, F. H. (2010). Relationships of the Big Five personality domains and facets to dimensions of the healthy personality. *Journal of Career Assessment, 18,* 147–160.

Bonito, J. A., & Sanders, R. E. (2011). The existential center of small groups: Member's conduct and interaction. *Small Group Research, 42,* 343–358.doi:10.1177/1046496410385472

Burlingame, G. M., Cox, J. C., Davies, R. D., Layne, C. M., & Gleave, R. (2011). The Group Selection Questionnaire: Further refinements in group member selection. *Group Dynamics: Theory, Research, and Practice, 15,* 60–74.

Burlingame, G. M., Fuhriman, A., & Johnson, J. E. (2001). Cohesion in group psychotherapy. *Psychotherapy, 38*(4), 373–379.

Burlingame, G. M., Fuhriman, A., & Mosier, J. (2003). The differential effectiveness of group psychotherapy: A meta-analytic perspective. *Group Dynamics: Theory, Research, and Practice, 7,* 3–12.

Burlingame, G. M., Kapetanovic, S., & Ross, S. (2005). Group psychotherapy. In S. S. Wheelan (Ed.), *The handbook of group research and practice* (pp. 387–406). Thousand Oaks, CA: Sage.

Capuzzi, D., Gross, D. R., & Stauffer, M. D. (2010). *Introduction to group work* (5th ed.). Denver, CO: Love.

Chapman, C. (2010). *Clinical prediction in group psychotherapy.* Unpublished doctoral dissertation, Brigham Young University, Provo, UT.

Chattopadhyay, P., Tluchowska, M., & George, E. (2004). Identifying the ingroup: A closer look at the influence of demographic dissimilarity on employee social identity. *Academy of Management Review, 29,* 180–202. doi:10.5465/amr.2004.12736071

Chukhray, N. I. (2012). Forming an ecosystem of innovation. *Economics of Development, 61,* 12–18.

Clarke, G. C., Lewinsohn, P., & Hops, H. (2000). *Leader's manual for adolescent groups: Adolescent coping with depression course.* Retrieved from http://www .kpchr.org/research/public/acwd/acwd.html

Comstock, D. L., Hammer, T. R., Strentzsch, J., Cannon, K., Parsons, J., & Custavo, S. (2008). Relational-cultural theory: A framework for bridging relational, multicultural, and social justice competencies. *Journal of Counseling & Development, 86,* 279–287.

Conyne, R. K. (1999). *Failures in group work: How we can learn from our mistakes.* Thousand Oaks, CA: Sage.

Conyne, R. K., & Cook, E. P. (Eds.). (2004). *Ecological counseling: An innovative approach to conceptualizing person-environment interaction.* Alexandria, VA: American Counseling Association.

Conyne, R. K., Crowell, J. L., & Newmeyer, M. D. (2008). *Group techniques: How to use them more purposefully.* Upper Saddle River, NJ: Pearson.

Conyne, R. K., Rapin, L. S., & Rand, J. M. (2008). A model for leading task groups. *Counseling and Human Development, 40,* 1–8.

Corey, M. S., Corey, G., & Corey, C. (2010). *Groups: Process and practice* (8th ed.). Belmont, CA: Brooks/Cole.

Council for Accreditation of Counseling and Related Educational Programs. (2009). *2009 standards.* Alexandria, VA: Author.

Crowell, J. L., Sebera, K. E., & Coaston, S. C. (2012). School counseling. In E. Cook (Ed.), *Understanding people in context: The ecological perspective in counseling* (pp. 207–227). Alexandria, VA: American Counseling Association.

Daner, D. E. (2009, November). If you build it, they will come: Building a robust group therapy program. *Commission for Counseling and Psychological Services Newsletter.*

Davies, D. R., Seaman, S., Burlingame, G. M., & Layne, C. (2002, February). *Selecting adolescents for trauma/grief-focused group psychotherapy.* Paper presented at the Annual Meeting of the American Group Psychotherapy Association, New Orleans, LA.

Delucia-Waack, J. L. (2004). Introduction to multicultural groups. In J. L. DeLucia-Waack, D. Gerrity, C. Kalodner, & T. Riva (Eds.), *Handbook of group counseling and psychotherapy* (pp. 167–168). Thousand Oaks, CA: Sage.

Delucia-Waack, J. L. (2006). *Leading psychoeducational groups for children and adolescents.* Thousand Oaks, CA: Sage.

Dutta, P. S., & Sen, S. (2003). Forming stable partnerships. *Cognitive Systems Research, 4,* 211–221.

Forsyth, D. (2010). *Group dynamics* (5th ed.). Belmont, CA: Wadsworth.

Fuhriman, A., & Burlingame, G. M. (2001). Group psychotherapy training and effectiveness. *International Journal of Group Psychotherapy, 51,* 399–416.

Gans, J. S., & Counselman, E. F. (2010). Patient selection for psychodynamic group psychotherapy: Practical and dynamic considerations. *International Journal of Group Psychotherapy, 60,* 197–220.

Gazda, G. M. (1989). *Group counseling: A developmental approach* (4th ed.). Boston: Allyn & Bacon.

Gladding, S. T. (2008). *Group work: A counseling specialty* (5th ed.). Upper Saddle River, NJ: Merrill/Prentice Hall.

Goldberg, L. (1999). A broad-bandwidth, public-domain, personality inventory measuring the lower-level facets of several Five-Factor Models. *Personality Psychology in Europe, 7,* 7–28.

Gosling, S. D., Rentfrow, P. J., & Swann, W. B., Jr. (2003). A very brief measure of the Big-Five personality domains. *Journal of Research in Personality, 37*, 504–528.

Grandison, A. L., Pharwaha, B. K., & Dratcu, L. (2009). The communication group: Bringing group psychotherapy back to acute in-patient psychiatry. *The Psychiatrist, 33*, 138–141.

Haley-Banez, L., Brown, S., Molina, B., D'Andrea, M., Arrendondo, P., Merchant, N., et al. (1999). Association for specialists in group work principles for diversity-competent group workers. *Journal for Specialists in Group Work, 24*(1), 7–14.

Hall, M. F., & Yager, G. G. (2012). Counseling in context: Counselor training. In E. P. Cook (Ed.), *Understanding people in context: The ecological counseling perspective* (pp. 279–296). Alexandria, VA: American Counseling Association.

Health Foundation of Greater Cincinnati. (2013). *What we fund.* Retrieved from https://www.healthfoundation.org/what-we-fund

Herner, L. M., & Higgins, K. (2000). Forming and benefiting from educator study groups. *Teaching Exceptional Children, 32*, 30–37.

Hilton, S., & Phillips, F. (2010). Instructor-assigned and student-selected groups: A view from inside. *Issues in Accounting Education, 25*, 15–33. doi:10.2308/iace.2010.25.1.15

Hines, P. L., & Fields, T. H. (2002). Pregroup screening issues for school counselors. *Journal for Specialists in Group Work, 27*(4), 358–376.

Jacobs, E. E., Masson, R. L., & Harvill, R. L. (2009). *Group counseling: Strategies and skills* (6th ed.). Belmont, CA: Thomson Higher Education.

Johnson, D. W., & Johnson, F. P. (2003). *Joining together: Group theory and group skills* (8th ed.). Boston: Pearson Education.

Kampmeier, C., & Simon, B. (2001). Individuality and group formation: The role of independence and differentiation. *Journal of Personality and Social Psychology, 81*, 448–462.

Knauss, L. K. (2006). Ethical issues in recordkeeping in group psychotherapy. *International Journal of Group Psychotherapy, 56*, 415–430.

Krogel, J., Beecher, M. E., Presnell, J., Burlingame, G., & Simonsen, C. (2009). The Group Selection Questionnaire: A qualitative analysis of potential group members. *International Journal of Group Psychotherapy, 59*, 529–542.

Kyprianidou, M., Demetriadis, S., Tsiatsos, T., & Pombortsis, A. (2012). Group formation based on learning styles: Can it improve students' teamwork? *Educational Technology Research and Development, 60*, 83–110.

Lasky, G. B., & Riva, M. T. (2006, October). Confidentiality and privileged communication in group psychotherapy. *International Journal of Group Psychotherapy, 56*(4), 455–476.

Laux, J. M., Smirnoff, J. B., Ritchie, M. H., & Cochrane, W. S. (2007). The effect of type of screening on the satisfaction of students in experiential counseling training groups. *Small Group Research, 38*, 289–300. doi:10.1177/1046496407300484

MacNair-Semands, R. R. (2002). Predicting attendance and expectations for group therapy. *Group Dynamics: Theory, Research, and Practice, 6*(3), 219–228.

MacNair-Semands, R. R. (2007). Attending to the spirit of social justice as an ethical approach in group therapy. *International Journal of Group Psychotherapy, 57*, 61–66.

Mojzisch, A., & Schulz-Hardt, S. (2010). Process gains in group decision making: A conceptual analysis, preliminary data, and tools for practitioners. *Journal of Managerial Psychology, 26*, 235–246. doi:10.1108/ 02683941111112668

National Association of Social Workers. (2008). *Code of ethics.* Washington, DC: Author. Retrieved from http://www.socialworkers.org/pubs/code/code.asp

National Board for Certified Counselors. (2005). *Code of ethics.* Greensboro, NC: Author. Retrieved from http://www.cce-global.org/Assets/ethics/nbcc -codeofethics-old.pdf

Nock, M. K., & Kurtz, S. M. (2005). Direct behavioral observation in school settings: Bringing science to practice. *Cognitive and Behavioral Practice, 12,* 359–370.

Ohio Revised Code, Chapter 4732.07. (2012). Retrieved from http://codes.ohio.gov/ orc/ 4732

Page, B. J. (2004). Online group counseling. In J. L. DeLucia-Waack, D. Gerrity, C. Kalodner, & M. Riva (Eds.), *Handbook of group counseling and psychotherapy* (pp. 609–620). Thousand Oaks, CA: Sage.

Perusse, R., Goodnough, G. G., & Lee, V. V. (2009). Group counseling in the schools. *Psychology in the Schools, 46,* 225–231.

Posthuma, B. W. (2002). *Small groups in counseling and therapy: Process and leadership* (4th ed.). Boston: Allyn & Bacon.

Price, J. R., & Price, A. R. (1999). Record keeping. In J. R. Price, D. R. Hescheles, & A. A. R. Price (Eds.), *A guide to starting psychotherapy groups* (pp. 43–46). San Diego, CA: Academic Press.

Rapin, L. S. (2004). Guidelines for ethical and legal practice in counseling and psychotherapy groups. In J. L. DeLucia-Waack, D. Gerrity, C. Kalodner, & M. Riva (Eds.), *Handbook of group counseling and psychotherapy* (pp. 151–165). Thousand Oaks, CA: Sage.

Rapin, L. S. (2011). Ethics, best practices and law in group counseling. In R. Conyne (Ed.), *The Oxford handbook of group counseling* (pp. 61–82). Oxford, UK: Oxford University Press.

Rapin, L. S. (2013). Guidelines for ethical and legal practice in counseling and psychotherapy groups. In J. L. Delucia-Waack, C. Kalodner, & M. Riva (Eds.), *Handbook of group counseling and psychotherapy* (2nd ed.). Thousand Oaks, CA: Sage.

Rapin, L. S., & Conyne, R. K. (2006). Best practices in group work. In J. Trotzer (Ed.), *The counselor and the group: Integrating theory, training, and practice* (4th ed., pp. 291–318). New York: Routledge.

Rapin, L. S., & Keel, L. P. (1998). ASGW best practice guidelines. *Journal for Specialists in Group Work, 23,* 237–244.

Renou, L. (2011). Group formation and governance. *Journal of Public Economic Theory, 13,* 595–630.

Riva, M. T. (2006, August). Group supervision: Current practices and results of a national survey. In M. Riva & L. Rapin (Co-chairs), *Taking a closer look at group supervision: Ethics, training, and research.* Presented at the American Psychological Association Convention, New Orleans.

Riva, M. T., Lippert, L., & Tackett, M. J. (2000). Selection practices of group leaders: A national survey. *Journal for Specialists in Group Work, 25,* 157–169.

Riva, M. T., Wachtel, M., & Lasky, G. (2004). Effective leadership in group counseling and psychotherapy: Research and practice. In J. L. Delucia-Waack, D. Gerrity, C. Kalodner, & M. Riva (Eds.), *Handbook of group counseling and psychotherapy.* (pp. 37–48). Thousand Oaks, CA: Sage.

Schachter, S. (1959). *The psychology of affiliation.* Stanford, CA: Stanford University Press.

Schmitt, M. T., Branscombe, N. R., Silvia, P. J., Garcia, D. M., & Spears, R. (2006). Categorizing at the group-level in response to intragroup social comparisons: A self-categorization theory integration of self-evaluation and social identity motives. *European Journal of Social Psychology, 36,* 297–314. doi:10.1002/ejsp.306

Shulman, L. (2010). *Dynamics and skills of group counseling.* Belmont, CA: Thompson, Brooks/Cole.

Singh, A. A., Merchant, N., Skudrzyk, B., & Ingene, D. (2012). *Association for Specialists in Group Work: Multicultural and social justice competence principles for group workers.* Retrieved from http://www.asgw.org/pdf/ASGW_MC_SJ_Priniciples_Final_ASGW.pdf

Spitz, H. I. (1996). *Group psychotherapy and managed mental health care: A clinical guide for providers.* New York: Brunner/Mazel.

Strauss, P., & U, A. (2007). Group assessments: Dilemmas facing lecturers in multicultural tertiary classrooms. *Higher Education Research and Development, 26,* 147–161.

Substance Abuse and Mental Health Services Administration. (2012). *Treatment improvement protocols.* Rockville, MD: Author.

Tang, M., & Bashir, H. (2012). Diversity from the ecological perspective. In. E. P. Cook (Ed.), *Understanding people in context: The ecological counseling perspective* (pp. 161–178). Alexandria, VA: American Counseling Association.

Thomas, R. V., & Pender, D. A. (2008). *Association for Specialists in Group Work: Best practice guidelines 2007 revisions.* Retrieved from http://asgw.org/pdf/Best_Practices.pdf

Tricare. (2012). Military benefits. Retrieved from http://www.military.com/benefits/tricare

Valenti, M. A., & Rockett, T. (2008). The effects of demographic differences on forming intragroup relationships. *Small Group Research, 39,* 179–202. doi:10.1177/1046496408315981

ValueOptions. (2012). *ABCs of mental health care: Treatment types; FAQS about group therapy* (Reprinted from American Group Psychotherapy Association, 2000). Retrieved from http://www.valueoptions.com/PMC_prototype/MemberConnect/mbr_faqsAboutGroupTherapy1.html

Whiston, S. C., & Quinby, R. F. (2009). Review of school counseling outcome research. *Psychology in the Schools, 46,* 267–272.

Wilkinson, I. A. G., & Fung, I. Y. Y. (2002). Small-group composition and peer effects. *International Journal of Educational Research, 37,* 425–447.

Wilson, F. R. (2004). Ecological psychotherapy. In R. K. Conyne & E. P. Cook (Eds.), *Ecological counseling: An innovative approach to conceptualizing person-environment interaction* (pp. 143–170). Alexandria, VA: American Counseling Association.

Wilson, F. R., Rapin, L. S., & Haley-Banez, L. (2000). *Professional standards for the training of group workers.* Retrieved from http://asgw.org/pdf/training_standards.pdf

Wilson, F. R., Rapin, L. S., & Haley-Banez, L. (2004). How teaching group work can be guided by foundational documents: Best practice guidelines, diversity principles, training standards. *Journal for Specialists in Group Work, 29,* 19–29.

Wittenbaum, G. M., Hollingshead, A. B., Paulus, P. B., Hirokawa, R. Y., Ancona, D. G., Peterson, R. S., et al. (2004). The functional perspective as a lens for understanding groups. *Small Group Research, 35,* 17–43. doi:10.1177/104649 6403259459

Wubbolding, R. E. (2000). *Reality therapy for the 21st century.* Philadelphia: Brunner-Routledge.

Yager, G. G. (2004). Training and supervision. In R. K. Conyne & E. P. Cook (Eds.), *Ecological counseling: An innovative approach to conceptualizing person-environment interaction* (pp. 171–193). Alexandria, VA: American Counseling Association.

Yalom, I. D. (1983). *Inpatient group psychotherapy.* New York: Basic Books.

Yalom, I. D. (with Leszcz, M.). (2005). *The theory and practice of group psychotherapy* (5th ed.). New York: Basic Books.

Zur, O. (2013). *Record keeping guidelines for psychologists, counselors, MFTs, social workers in private psychotherapy and counseling practice.* Sonoma, CA: Zur Institute. Retrieved from http://www.zurinstitute.com/recordkeepingguidelines .html

Index _____

American College Personnel
    Association (ACPA), 7
American Counseling Association
    (ACA), 6–7
American Group Psychotherapy
    Association (AGPA), 10–11,
    27, 29
American Mental Health Counselors
    Association (AMHCA), 7–8
American Psychological
    Association, 9
American School Counselor
    Association, 8
Association for Specialists in Group
    Work (ASGW), 10–11, 31
Association for the Advancement
    of Social Work with Groups
    (AASWG), 10
Attachment style model, 31

Behavior sampling, 34–35
Best practice guidelines, 10–11
Big Five Personality
    Inventory-Short, 42

Case examples
    study group formation, 51–56
    working with street women, 56–60
Certified Group Therapist
    credentials, 11
Choice theory, 22
Client, defined, 6–7
Client records, 18–19
Closed groups, 45–47
Coleadership, 17
Composing, 5, 45–49
    case examples, 56, 60
    open *vs.* closed groups, 45–47
Conceptual support, 5–6

Confidentiality
    document standards, 6–9
    limits, 21, 47
Conscientiousness, 42–43
Context of group, 3
Council for Accreditation of
    Counseling and Related
    Educational Programs (CACREP),
    10–11
Counseling documents, 6–9
Countertransference, 39–40
Cultural bias, 20
Cultural influences, 31–32

Demeanor subscale, 40–41
Demographics of group members, 3
Disclosure by group member, 21
Diversity of group, 20, 22, 31
Documents, ethics and training
    standards, 5–12

Ecological background, case examples,
    53–54, 57–59
Ecological checklist, 47–49
Ecology of a group, 2–4, 51–52
Ethics, 20–21
Ethics documents, 5–12
Evaluation, 19–20
Expectancy subscale, 40

Formation. *See* Group formation
    process

Group composition, 45
    See also Composing
Group development, 12
Group formation process
    applying the steps, 60–62
    factors affecting, 3–4

introduction to, 1–2
overview of steps in, 4–5
Group leaders
  information about, 36
  shortage of, 23
Group schedule, 14
Group Selection Questionnaire (GSQ),
  36–37, 40–41
Group specialty documents, 10–12
Group Therapy Questionnaire,
  37, 41

Heterogeneous groups, 45–46
Homogeneous groups, 45–46
Humana Military, 27

Informed consent, 47
Instruments, selection, 40–44
Insurance companies, 16, 26–27
Interaction Process Analysis, 35
Internet culture, 21
Interviews, 32, 33–34, 37

Learning exercises, 12, 24, 30, 37,
  44, 47–49, 60–62
Learning style inventory, 37
Length of sessions, 14

Machines, 19–20, 59
Managed-care insurance companies,
  26–27
Management support, 15–17,
  54, 57–58
Manpower, 17, 54, 58
Marketing, 4–5, 25–28
  case examples, 55. 59–60
  to managed care, 26–27
  planning groups, 25–26
  site-specific variables, 27–28
Materials, 17–19, 54, 58
Methods, 19–20, 55, 58–59
Minors
  recruiting, 29–30
  screening, 35–36
Money, 20, 55, 59
Multiculturalism, 31–32

National Association of Social
  Workers, 9
National Board for Certified
  Counselors, 8
National Registry of Certified Group
  Psychotherapists, 10

Ohio laws and regulations, 13
Online groups, 21
Open groups, 45–47
Organization mission, 15
Organizing, 4, 13–24
  case examples, 53–55,
    57–59
  ecological checklist, 47–49
  professional context, 13–14
  regulatory requirements,
    13–14
  resource inventory, 14–24.
    See also Resources
Orientation to group, 46–47

Participation subscale, 40
Personal identity, 24
Personality traits, 41–43
Physical location, 17–18
Planning for group formation, 1–2
Planning groups, 25–26
Pregroup meeting, for
  orientation, 47
Pregroup phase, 11
Printed materials, 18
Professional context, 13–14
Professional identity for leaders, 22
Psychology document, 9–10

Reality therapy, 22
Recruiting, 4–5, 28–30
  case examples, 55, 59–60
  of minors, 29–30
Referrals, 29
Regulatory requirements, 13–14
Relational demography, 3
Research, 19–20
Research-based screening instruments,
  36–37
Resources, 14–24, 54–55, 57–59
  ethics, 20–21
  machines, 19–20, 59
  management support, 15–17,
    54, 57–58
  manpower, 17, 54, 58
  materials, 17–19, 54, 58
  methods, 19–20, 55, 58–59
  money, 20, 55, 59
  scope of practice, 21–23
  six Ms, 15
  supervision, 23–24
  time, 14–15, 54, 57
Role play, 33

Scope of practice, 21–23
Screening, 5, 6, 31–37
    behavior sampling, 34–35
    case examples, 55, 60
    interviews, 32, 33–34
    and managed-care companies, 26
    of minors, 35–36
    role play, 33
Screening instruments, research-based,
    36–37
Seating arrangements, 18
Selecting, 5, 39–44
    case examples, 55–56, 60
Selection instruments, 40–44
Self-categorization theory, 3
Self-Compassion Scale, 41–42
Site-specific variables, 27–28

Social comparison theory, 31
Social justice, 32
Social work document, 9
Standards documents, 5–12
Supervision, 7, 23–24
Synomorphy, 17–18

Theoretical orientation, 22
Theoretical support, 5–6
Therapeutic factors, 32–33
Time, 14–15, 54, 57
Training, 7

ValueOptions, 27

Yalom's 11 therapeutic factors,
    32–33

About the Authors _____

Lynn S. Rapin, PhD, has strong ties to group work, having served as president of the Association for Specialists in Group Work (ASGW) and as treasurer and president of Division 49 of the American Psychological Association (Group Psychology and Group Psychotherapy). She also coauthored the ASGW *Best Practice Guidelines* (1998) and ASGW training standards (2000). Lynn consults with task groups in her practice and provides management coaching, in addition to her psychology practice with adolescents and adults. Lynn's specialty areas are group ethics and best practices, program development and evaluation, and group organization and team effectiveness. She had the pleasure of teaching for 25 years in a master's and doctoral counseling program and, now, serving as colleague to her coauthor, Jeri L. Crowell.

Jeri L. Crowell, EdD, is a licensed professional counselor in Georgia, certified in reality therapy, and is a faculty member of the William Glasser Institute. Dr. Crowell is also a National Certified Counselor and a Distance Credentialed Counselor. Dr. Crowell is a Core Faculty member at Capella University in the master's mental health counseling program and the doctoral counselor education and supervision program. Her research interests are largely qualitative and include group work, crisis assessment and intervention, suicide prevention and survivor counseling, wellness and spirituality, and the application of reality therapy/choice theory in counseling settings.

⑤SAGE research**methods**

The essential online tool for researchers from the world's leading methods publisher

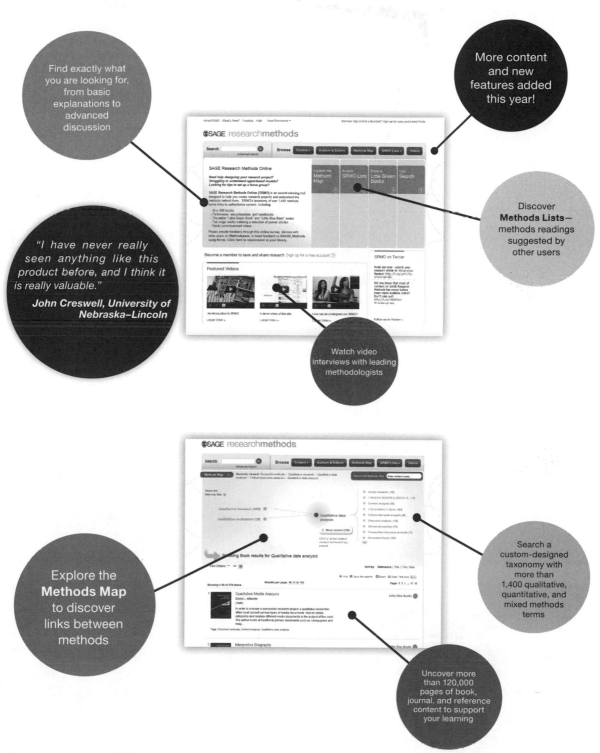

Find exactly what you are looking for, from basic explanations to advanced discussion

More content and new features added this year!

Discover **Methods Lists**— methods readings suggested by other users

"*I have never really seen anything like this product before, and I think it is really valuable.*"

John Creswell, University of Nebraska–Lincoln

Watch video interviews with leading methodologists

Explore the **Methods Map** to discover links between methods

Search a custom-designed taxonomy with more than 1,400 qualitative, quantitative, and mixed methods terms

Uncover more than 120,000 pages of book, journal, and reference content to support your learning

Find out more at
www.sageresearchmethods.com

WITHDRAWN